CW00467632

THE LIGHT AT THE END OF THE TUNNEL

By

HARRY HONE

THE LIGHT AT THE END OF THE TUNNEL

Copyright © 1986 by Harry Hone. ----

All rights reserved. No part of this book except for brief passages in articles and/or reviews that refer to the author and/or the publisher may be reproduced without written permission of the author.

Library of Congress Number 79-55362

ISBN 09601168-4-2

Publisher & Distributor
AMERICAN BIO CENTER
P.O.Box 473, Williamsburg, Va 23187

A FEW HEARTFELT WORDS FROM
<u>THE WIFE</u>
OF THE AUTHOR OF
"THE LIGHT AT THE END OF THE TUNNEL"

From the minute we are born, we are beginning to die. When we think about that as we grow older we know it is true and accept it as a rueful reality.

We also hope the process of *gradually* dying, inevitable as it is will be long and enjoyable.

But the length of our life depends on the parts of our body lasting the course, and *not* coming to a sudden and premature end.

<u>THE HEART OF THE MATTER.</u>

However, this can happen. It did indeed happen to the author. Without warning his heart stopped beating for two minutes. For two minutes he left his body—the "house" he lived in, and journeyed back in time to where he originated and lived *before* he entered his body at the moment of birth.

This book is an account of his unique odyssey to where we all go when we "die", and an epic revelation of the "place" where we all come from in the "beginning".

Since we *all* rely on our heart continuing to beat in order that we may continue to live, you—the reader are no different than any other mortal.

From this viewpoint alone, if *your* heart were to stop beating you would find yourself taking the same journey the author traveled.

His book, "The Light At The End Of The Tunnel" will give you a unique preview of what *you* may expect on your journey after you leave this life. Read and enjoy.

(Every word my husband wrote immediately following his "near death" experience is a verbatim record of exactly what happened to him while "out of his body". In point of fact this "book" is nothing more than his typewritten <u>original manuscript</u> made into the book you now hold in your hand. Not a single word has been changed or "improved" upon.)

LOIS (LOU) HONE

THE TRUTH IS-----IN ONE WAY OR ANOTHER EVERYONE IS LOOKING FOR WHAT MY HUSBAND DISCOVERED AREN'T THEY?

AND THAT IS------
"THE LIGHT AT THE END OF THE TUNNEL"

AN EARLIER LIFE CHANGING EPOCH

We were "runaway lovers". I was nineteen, Harry my husband to be was 22, We lived in London, England and my parents thought I was too young to get married.
So we eloped.
I travelled to Scotland in order to become a Scottish Citizen. This meant a stay of three weeks. After that time, Scottish law decreed I was now a "Scot", and could determine my own future.
This included the right to get married.

GRETNA GREEN

Gretna Green, a small community near Dumfries (in Scotland) was world famous way back then as the locale for quick marriages.
The local blacksmith was an ordained minister. Marriages were solemnized over the blacksmith's <u>anvil</u>. It was romantic, exciting and <u>legal</u>.
It was right there, in Bonnie Scotland after a whirlwind elopement, that Harry and I cemented a "never to be parted" union that up until the time of his "near death" experience had produced three wonderful children and a solid "life long" marriage.

BUT HIS "HEART ATTACK"----
looked like this might be the end of it.
But It Wasn't.
To get the whole story----you must read the rest of the book.
I was a witness to how it all started-----and was there in the hospital when his "out of the body" experiences were recounted to his doctor and startled nurses.
I was just as amazed as they were to hear what happened after he left his body.
I think you will be too as you learn what happened when his journey into "another dimension" took him unerringly to the "THE LIGHT AT THE END OF THE TUNNEL"

Lovingly,

Lois (Lou) Hone.

THE LIGHT AT THE END OF THE TUNNEL
Third Printing March 1996

COLOPHON PAGE

The Light At The End Of The Tunnel.

A Limited Manuscript Edition

The author's signature below testifies that this bound book is a
faithful copy of his original manuscript.

Author

Dedicated to

my dear wife Lou,

Dr. McCormick and Dr. Horgan,

the

entire medical staff at

Riverside Hospital, Newport News,

Virginia,

and

all those searching for
THE LIGHT AT THE END OF THE TUNNEL

TABLE OF CONTENTS

ILLUSTRATED WITH 3 PAGES OF PHOTOGRAPHS

ADDENDUM, QUESTIONS AND ANSWERS

WHILE "OUT OF MY BODY"
HERE IS ONE OF MY
EARLY MEMORIES---RE-VISITED IN THE BEYOND

MY FATHER HARRY (in British Army Uniform World War 1)

MY MOTHER ADA (the most wonderful mother a son ever had)

ME AT AGE THREE (I'm the one in front with the curly hair)

WHEN WE BEGIN LIFE AS A CHILD, HOW CAN WE TELL WHAT IS AHEAD OF US???

THE LIGHT AT THE END OF THE TUNNEL TELLS THE MOST POTENT PART OF MINE.

THIS MAN CAME

BACK FROM THE DEAD

THE "SCENE" FROM ABOVE.
THIS IS EXACTLY WHAT I
SAW WHILE I WAS OUT OF
MY BODY.

TEN YEARS LATER—
BACK IN MY BODY—
AND FEELING FINE.

DATELINE BIRMINGHAM, ENGLAND

THIS IS THE "EVE" OF THE TENTH ANNIVERSARY OF MY "DEATH".

To celebrate it I am putting down on paper a personal,
eye-witness account of the unique events and experiences
which occurred before, during, and after I saw

"THE LIGHT AT THE END OF THE TUNNEL"

and came

"BACK FROM THE DEAD."

Since most people believe you can't get out of this
world "alive," it's my hope that the story of what happened
to me will

1/ Give new meaning to your "life"

2/ Take the "sting" out of your thoughts

about "death."

BECAUSE WE DO INDEED GET OUT OF THIS WORLD ALIVE

Bon Voyage!

A LETTER FROM THE DOCTOR

It has been said that the fear of the unknown is perhaps the worst fear. There is a certain helplessness in unknown surroundings, unfamiliar faces - a loss of control. To be seized suddenly in the middle of the night with chest pain, to be brought to the hospital under urgent circumstances for help and diagnosis, such was the plight of Mr. Harry Hone on the evening of December 16, 1976. It was in the active and exhaustive emergency room of Riverside Hospital that I first met this extra-ordinarily perceptive and sensitive individual.

He was referred by his private physician from an outlying rural area for evaluation of chest pain. It had occurred early in the morning and was described as oppressive and vise-like. Initial examination, laboratory studies and electrocardiogram were normal. He was transferred to the Coronary Care Unit for observation and monitoring. The possibility of an acute myocardial infarction had to be considered.

Within 90 minutes of arrival in the Coronary Care Unit, he developed a marked slowing of his heart rate, which was recorded on the monitor and observed by the nurse. Emergency measures were instituted at once, with prompt restoration of a normal heartbeat.

The few seconds in which these activities took place were to have a profound influence on Harry Hone. The admixture of events which brought him to this place in these circumstances, new and unexplainable symptoms, the knowledge that he was suddenly in a Coronary Care Unit with all of its bizarre equipment and gadgetry, the possibility that his doctors were convinced he was having a heart attack and could die, and finally the resuscitation efforts on his behalf with his partial awareness--this experience provided him with the material to write this book.

The complete recovery of an individual from an illness involves not only the recouping of physical strength, but also the mental understanding and spiritual acceptance of the problem. Such has been the toil of the author. It is my professional opinion that Mr. Hone has achieved a complete recovery.

Hugh Bernard McCormick, M.D.,
F.A.C.C.

A NOTE FROM THE AUTHOR

The words you will read in this book are the exact words used in preparing my manuscript. In point of fact, the book IS my manuscript made and bound into book form. The book therefore is a replica in every way of my manuscript manufactured into a book without change, modification or alteration in any detail of the original written word.

I waited ten years before presenting the manuscript in book form to to the public in order that my odyssey from life to death, and back again from death to life could not be interpreted as a passing mirage or a quirk of nature.

The information I had to give was pent up inside and it was with great difficulty and patience that I managed to suppress it.

I had two principal reasons for waiting. One was to establish by a considerable TIME factor the lasting effect of my "return". The second was to demonstrate in real life terms the efficacy and reality of the floodtide of voiceless instructions I received from the beyond while "out of my body".

I make one appeal to the reader. When you read the "words", remember they are NOT the things, events, or experiences they attempt to explain or describe. They are just "words".

In and of themselves they have no more power to cure or change conditions than do the "words" on the label of a pharmacy medicine container. It's what's INSIDE that counts.

When you read the "words", go "inside". That's where you'll find the reality of cure and change and also the answers to the mysteries of "life" and "death"

You have ALL the answers within you.

OUT OF THE MOUTHS OF BABES————

Children say some unexpected things. I heard one child remark——"Are you sure you grown-ups know what you are doing?".
A good question.
Do we?

Chapter One

"EXODUS"

My heart stopped beating at exactly 11:27 a.m. It was Thursday, December 16. It was a first time experience for me. It was also totally unexpected and totally devastating.

But that's not all. It was also dramatically instructive and unbelievably illuminating.

During this interval of "cardiac arrest", (as it was described in my medical records) I discovered that any notion I may have entertained that I, Harry Hone, personally powered my "life", was an utter illusion.

I quickly became aware that the power that pulled the "plug" from my life source was the same power which created and centered the life source itself.

When the energising flow of life current ceased, my heart function ceased with it. I left the world of "substance" I knew, and entered another world I didn't know.

This new environment appeared to be a "limitless dark void" where miraculously I found it possible to "see" without the stimulus of what we call "light".

It was a different kind of darkness, blacker than the blackest night. However, I could see far more clearly "there" than I had ever been able to see "here".

But let me get back to the beginning, to the series of events that led to this unplanned and unanticipated experience.

On Wednesday December 15, I had retired for the
night after what had been a usual kind of day. I looked
the same as I usually looked, and felt the same as I
usually felt. Usual and normal ---- and ready for a
night's sleep.

Then, at 4:00 a.m. on the morning of December 16,
something very unusual and abnormal took place.

I had awakened from a deep sleep and walked to the
bathroom, a distance of some twenty feet. Then from
"nowhere", and with breathtaking suddenness, I received
what felt like a vicious kick in the chest. The impact
was like a ponderous blow from the savage stomp of an
elephant.

The breath left my body, I became weak and limp, and
fell to the floor.

I clutched at my heart in a futile effort to ward
off the next assault. This came in the form of a slow
but relentless kind of torture. It seemed as though a
huge steel vice had been fastened on my heart, and a
giant with superhuman strength was squeezing the life
out of me.

Powerless to resist or escape from the torture, and
with what seemed like the last breath I would ever take,
I called out to my wife -- "Lou, please help me".

Miraculously she heard my barely audible voice,
and flew to my rescue.

Within seconds I felt her warm hands massaging my heart through the walls of my chest.

Under the influence of her loving care and words of unbelieving concern, I regained some measure of confidence. The excruciating pain began to evaporate as she continued with instinctive but untutored first aid.

I was unable to speak, but voicelessly conveyed my gratitude through my eyes. I am convinced that her prompt action in those first early moments saved my life. As she continued her attempts at first aid, I began to breathe more rythmically --- but still very shallowly.

The agony inflicted on my heart from that "one--two" assault slowly faded, only to be replaced with cold, shivering "sweats." Lou told me later that my face was ashen gray. She was scared and puzzled, but bravely kept her composure.

To me, lying there helpless on the floor, she represented LIFE. My deepest desire was to hang on to her -- and I prayed for the strength to do so.

As the color slowly came back to my face, and I began to feel and look more "alive", she decided to leave me in order to call the doctor. It was now almost 4:30, and within thirty minutes Dr. Hudgins who practiced medicine in nearby Mathews made his appearance. My wife quickly gave him the details of my sudden collapse, and he examined me right where I lay on the bathroom floor. His

verdict, in concerned but certain tones, was that I
had suffered a heart attack.

Leaving me lying prone where I had fallen, he
called the rescue squad.

I was a very passive spectator. Still too weak to
move or even speak, my mind was alertly conscious of
what was going on around me. By the time the ambulance
arrived, some strength had returned to my body, and I
could talk.

This was progress. I felt the worst was over. As
the forty-five minute ride to Riverside Hospital in
Newport News brought me closer to more organized medical
help, I mentally noted that the ambulance needed new
springs -- or the road needed repairs. I marvelled at
the irrelevance of my thought processes, and patiently
resigned myself to what would happen next.

I didn't have long to wait.

Once inside the hospital emergency ward, doctors
appeared like magic. With professional speed and alert
attention, they carried out further medical checks. In
answers to their questioning, I gave them the same account
of the sequel of events my wife had given to Dr. Hudgins.
As I recounted the details, I had the distinct impression
I was talking about something that had happened to someone else.

Everything seemed to be so unreal and impossible. I

had heard of other people having heart attacks -- but never once dreamed it could possibly happen to me.

Still in the emergency room, the doctors left me under the care of a nurse. This gave me a respite from further questions and a chance to collect my scattered thoughts.

At this point my wife arrived. For a few moments we held hands. I felt "safe" again. However, we were interrupted by the arrival of still another physician who asked me to sign some official looking papers. Immediately after this matter of protocol was over, I was propelled into the "Cardiac Care Unit".

I made the transition from a mobile stretcher into an immobile bed without mishap. An attentive nurse took my blood pressure, and I was "wired" to an electrocardio-graph.

Later I was asked still more questions. As I responded I became aware that not only was I the victim of the "attack", I was also the raconteur.

As a new patient in the Cardiac Care Unit, instructions were given to me as to what I could and couldn't do. I was told to "press the red button" if I needed immediate help. To be perfectly frank, I was only remotely aware of these verbal orders. When the test came later, the details of what action I should take in an emergency were

the farthest thing from my mind. At this point, I still
felt tired and battered. However, my wife informed me
I did look a little better.

In the usual run of things, visitors were allowed
a ten minute stay with the patients. By this time,
however, Lou had been at my bedside about four hours. The
entire staff at Riverside Hospital was professionally
attentive and wonderfully understanding. After a con-
ference with the attending physicians, she advised me
she would have to leave in order that I could have
"complete rest". I was disappointed, but felt relieved
when she told me she'd be back again in a couple of
hours or so.

She kissed me gently -- and left.

It was now about 11:00 a.m. I had been in the hospital approximately five hours.

Then at 11:27 a.m. it happened.

I can recall the circumstances clearly. First I
began to feel nauseated, and tried to sit up in bed. I
succeeded in doing this, but immediately began to feel
worse. I became awfully weak -- and felt myself "slip-
ping away".

It didn't feel at all like "fainting". Fainting feels
like "giving up". This felt like being "taken away".

I got the impression I was leaving on a journey to
an unknown destination. I felt sure I was going "some-

where else." With my last breath I called out --
"something is wrong -- I am going," -- and I went.

I discovered later, the patient in the adjacent
bed had called out to the attending nurses. Two of them
immediately rushed to my bedside. The doctors weren't
far behind.

The medical terminology for their concern was described as a "cardiac arrest".

In other words, my heart had stopped beating. I had
left for a brief visit to "another world".

What I discovered there is the basis for this book,
but before I get to that, let me share with you what
happened when I "came back".

"Back From The Dead"

The first thing I saw on my return was what appeared
to be an "angel". However unlike any angel I had ever
heard of, this one was beating in a most unangelic way on
my chest with her fists. The "angel" was a nurse. Her
name I learned later was Eileen Smith. I don't suppose I
will ever forget her name. Another "angel" was about to
give me artificial resuscitation by means of a plastic
mouthpiece. This was another nurse. Her name was Terri
Tapscott. The first "words" I heard were "thank God I've
got him back -- thank God I've got him back".

At this moment I knew I had "returned". Like the
nurse said -- I had "come back".

If I could have spoken at that moment, I would have said "thank God" too. Since speaking was an impossibility with a plastic mouthpiece in the way, I brought up my hand and brushed it away. In retrospect, I remember it flying across the room and landing on the floor with a loud "click".

I became aware there were several people gathered round my bed. The cardiologists in attendance, Drs. Horgan and McCormick, and both nurses looked relieved. I felt somewhat bewildered. I tried to convey my thanks through my eyes. Once again I found myself breathless and physically weak. However, my mental processes seemed as alert as ever, and while I lay there recovering from my experiences, I started to try to put all the jumbled pieces together.

Fortunately, my visit to the "other world" had been brief, but I will always remember the "scenery". At the moment of my departure I was "pulled" away from the "here and now" and found myself travelling at lightning speed into the "future".

The power that pulled me was irresistable, and strangely enough I had no desire to resist. I went willingly.

The "force" that controlled the direction of my journey was delightfully persuasive. I actually found myself looking forward to it. Its gentle pulsating power propelled me firmly and unerringly into a tunnel-like black void, where in spite of the impenetrable darkness I could "see". At the end of the tunnel,"I" emerged into an indescribable, effulgently pure white world of "light".

I had the feeling that I was still "me" --- but without the inertia and weight of my body. I felt wondrously at peace, and had an almost euphoric anticipation as to what I might "see" next. All was "dark" -- yet I could "see". It was at that moment I realized that "I" was the "light" that <u>enabled</u> me to "see".

My body was "there" -- and "I" was "here". I became alertly aware of the separated difference. Then, after learning all I am about to share with you, I was abruptly brought back to this world of "substance", the world we have come to accept as the "real" world. Perhaps reading this book will change your mind about this. The experiences it describes certainly changed mine.

"Death" Is One Of The "Experiences" Of "Life"

Contrary to popular belief, I found the "process of death" a delightful experience. I discovered the "place of death" to be one of absolute "peace". It was a welcome release from the trauma of what we call "life". During my brief stay there, I developed a love for it I will always find difficult to explain. When it came time to return -- I was reluctant to leave.

You can take my word for it, "this world" as we live it -- is the battleground on which we fight an unending "war".

The "other world" is the place where we find the "peace that passeth all understanding".

I know -- I've been there!

The News Breaks

News travels fast in a small town, and it wasn't
long after my release from the hospital that my phone
began to ring. Three newspapers wanted to do a "story".
At that time, I was in no mood to talk about my experience and I politely but firmly refused to be interviewed. However, one reporter persisted. Her name was
Virginia Gabrielle, and she worked for the Daily Press.
She called me several times and explained that my story
would be helpful to others. I made several proper and
personal excuses why I should not go along with her suggestion -- but relented when she pointed out that an increas-
ing number of people were interested in the subject of
"dying". They wanted to know "what it was like", and since
I had "come back" and could tell what it was like -- perhaps I ought to share my experience with others.

I agreed to an interview after she promised she
would handle the story with due regard for my "feelings"
about "going public" on a subject I had until then considered
purely private. The following is a reprint of her story
as it appeared in the newspaper.

Afterwards, when I reviewed it, I felt she had
handled the matter with great sensitivity and understanding.

During the interview, she displayed an admirable degree
of patience as I stumbled over words that seemed so inadequate. I find it just as difficult now as I write this

book, as I did then.

The following is her account of our interview.

Life Has A Special Meaning For Harry Hone

By Virginia Gabriele
Staff Reporter

WILLIAMSBURG - Life has an extra special meaning for Harry Hone. He believes he has come back from the dead.

Hone is a middle-aged man with a clipped British accent and an affectionate manner.

But words fail him as he tries to describe an experience that has no equal.

It was an experience that convinced him that the spirit or person Harry Hone is a tiny speck or spark of light that lives inside the body known as Harry Hone. When that body dies, the light will live on.

Hone was not an overly religious man. And he was proud that his disciplined regimen has kept him fit and trim.

In fact, until that day in December when his heart stopped, he had "never been sick" in his life.

In answer to my questions, Hone talked about his experience.

His face and hands moved expressively with each thought, as a mime making words superfluous.

The attack in the early morning hours of Dec. 16 was a "total, all encompassing surprise".

"I felt good. I looked good. I didn't see anything wrong with myself when I shaved in the morning".

Hone had gotten up at 4 a.m. and was in the bathroom when he suddenly felt like he had been kicked in the chest by an elephant. That was quickly followed by the feeling that his heart was being crushed in a vise.

His wife Lois heard his weak cries and revived him by massaging his chest.

Within an hour the doctor arrived at the Mathews County home, and by 6 a.m. the Mathews County Rescue Squad had taken him to Riverside Hospital in Newport News.

Lois sat with him in the cardiac care unit where he was connected to several machines until 11 a.m. At that time he felt "pretty bewildered, but OK, just weak". However, he didn't want her to leave.

The narrative grows slower. He leans back in the chair and looks into the distance, carefully choosing words that best approximate his experience and his gestures become more expressive.

At 11:27 a.m., Hone said he sat up in bed and called out "Something is going wrong. I'm going."

Unaware of desperate efforts by nurses to revive him, Hone felt his spirit being drawn out of his body by a very powerful but gentle magnet or force.

"I was aware that I, me, was on a journey and had left my body."

This force then drew him down a "very very black tunnel." He felt pleasant and warm and was willing to go.

The tunnel opened up into a great area of indescribable white light, and Hone realized he was an integral part of it.

He also realized that Harry Hone consists of a "tiny speck or spark of light" and that light had left its body or house.

There were no voices or words or people, but somehow Hone got messages and information.

His life flashed by in the "blink of an eyelash" and something "taught me about myself".

Coming back to the present, Hone says that "if this is what happens when people die, they have absolutely nothing to be afraid of...The actual division between being alive in the body and being somewhere else is painless and rather pleasant."

There were other messages or feelings. Hone was uncertain whether to discuss them, saying they sound unorthodox.

Hone got the impression there is no <u>geographic</u> heaven and hell.

"We build our own heavens and hells right here in our own lives."

But at the same time, there are no permanent saints and no permanent sinners. Everyone is equal. Even the "saddest example of humanity can become the greatest".

Hone believes he came back because he had

"unfinished business to complete".

As he re-entered the dark area and travelled back through the tunnel, he saw a nurse beating on his chest with her fist.

Hone said, "I had no trouble rejoining my body."

Upon His Return

He heard the nurse say "thank God I've got him back", and then his arm flung away the plastic resuscitator in his throat.

As modern medicine brings more and more people back from the brink of death, more people are experiencing similar vivid experiences.

Like Hone, many are reluctant to talk about it for fear of ridicule.

Dr. Raymond A. Moody, Jr. has recounted hundreds of such tales in a recent best-selling book "Life After Life".

Hone said "something stopped" him when he tried to buy Moody's book, and he couldn't bring himself to attend a recent lecture by Moody at the College of William and Mary.

Moody has found parallels for such experiences in early literature, including the Bible, the works of Plato, writings from Tibet and Sweden.

Moody draws no conclusions about life after death in his book, but he does say such experiences "have very profound implications for what every one of us is doing with his life".

Hone says he is writing down his entire experience, trying to remember "every salient point".

He encountered no other problems during a brief stay in the hospital, and says he feels fine again.

Heightening the peculiarity of the whole experience was his doctor's pronouncement Jan. 25th. Hone had not had a heart attack as everyone thought. His medical history now shows only " chest pains from an unknown cause".

Hone says the profoundly moving experience has made several changes in his life.

He can no longer watch television shows depicting violence.

But most important, his attitude toward life has changed.

"I have a much greater reverence for life and people," he says. "It sounds sticky, but I've got the feeling I could put my arms around everyone."

WORDS - WORDS - WORDS

At this point, I think it might be helpful to your understanding of what follows, if you re-read the front section of the book dealing with "words".

Remember, the "words" I use are not the things, events or experiences they describe or explain. They are, at best, poor substitutes for the "real thing".

The time I was separated from my body was spent in complete silence. It was during this silence that I learned much of what I am sharing with you in this book. I learned that "silence" gives birth to sound. Words are merely a vocal expression of what the silence is already telling us. Hardly anyone listens to the silence anymore. In this book, the silent spaces between the words are at the very least as important as the words themselves. To fully understand what I am trying to describe, listen to the silence as well as the sound. Without silence, there could be no sound. Without silence, there could be no music.

When the pianist plays, there are times when he strikes the notes and there are times when he doesn't.

Both are of equal importance to the melody. The "silence" between them is what makes beautiful music -- and music beautiful. All sound and no silence results in a meaningless cacophony of discordant "noise".

I'd like to share the silences with you as well as the

sound. This is the only way we can tune out the "noise".
Noise is indicative of "this world".

Silence is the unmistakable hallmark of the "other
world".

This simple truth, and all that follows, is a faithful report of what I learned in the silence of my absence
from my body.

Chapter Two

REVELATION

"You" Are Not Your Body

Ever since man began to "live", he has wondered what it is like to "die". Being the reasoning creature he is, this comes as no surprise.

Because so few people die and then come back to tell what it's like, details of the experience are hard to come by. We usually settle for what other people "think" it's like. For the most part, we listen to the words and thoughts of religionists, theologians and philosophers. When I "died", I discovered that their "surface" explanations do indeed bear some relationship to the actual truth.

But right there at the surface, is where the relationship ends. I discovered when I "died", that in order to understand "death", you must first learn to understand "life".

You must know where you came from, why you're here, and where you go when you "die".

But that's not all.

You must also learn who you are, what you are, and what you will, in "time", become.

These are some of the things I will share with you in this book. So, let's begin at the beginning, from the

moment I left "this world", and entered the "other"
world. Let me share with you the process of "life" and
"death" as I discovered it to be.

It's John Brown's Body That Lies
a "Mouldering in the Grave" -- Not John Brown

First, "you" are not your body. You live in your body
in much the same way you live in your house. When your
house becomes old, dilapidated, or uninhabitable, you
move out.

When your body becomes old, dilapidated, or uninhabitable, you move out of that also.

It's just that simple.

I also learned that your body won't "do" anything
unless "you" tell it to. As a matter of fact, when you
leave your body -- as I did, it just lies where you left
it -- and does nothing at all.

People will say you are "dead", but that's not true.
"You" are the "life", and you have left. "You" are not dead.
It's your <u>body</u> that's "dead".

As a direct result of your departure, your lungs stop
functioning, your heart stops beating, your "fire" goes
out, and your body grows cold.

At this point, <u>it's not your body</u>. It's the body
you <u>used</u> to live in - unless you come back as I did, and

re-claim it. If you leave for good -- other people will
decide what to do with the body you have just given up.
You have moved out, relinquished title to it, and have
no further control over its future.

"You" Are Not Your "Body"

In "real" life, the following would be a good comparison. If you decided to leave your house for the
last time, you would probably snap off the light before
you left, and if the furnace was on, you'd turn that off
too. Like your body, your house would become empty, dark,
and soon grow cold.

On your way out, you might also walk down the garden
path to the gate. Once there, you may decide to take one
last final look at the house you had lived in for so many
years.

It would still be there, right where you had left
it, but "you" wouldn't be inside. --You'd be on the outside looking in.

That's exactly what it's like when you leave your
body. You will probably turn around to take one last
look at it -- like I did. It will still be there, inert
and lifeless. It would appear very much as it does when
you are sleeping - but there would be a distinct difference.

"You" are not in residence. "You" have left. Your
body, like your house, is empty. Its temporary resident

has moved out for the last time. You will return to where you came from. Your body will return to where it came from.

"This" World - and the "Other" World

When I looked back, my body was lying on the hospital bed surrounded by doctors and nurses. Watching, I could "see" them feverishly working, trying to induce me to come back. In a detached but still interested way, I "saw" all this from a vantage point outside my body. They were frantic -- I was calm. They were in "this" world. I was in the "other".

I didn't feel at all strange in my new environment. Somehow everything seemed normal and natural. In the brief passage of time I was away, I discovered there are two worlds. The world of the senses, and the world of the spirit. "Spirit" is a poor choice of words, but I can't think of any other word to use. All I can tell you is -- that whatever word is used, it is pitifully inadequate to describe the world we all go to when we "die".

In my conscious but apparently invisible state, I knew I was still in the world -- but not "of" it.

I saw everything that was going on without being an active and recognizable participant.

It was something like being at the movies. I could see the actors playing their parts as though from a seat in a darkened theater.

I could see them--but it was obvious they couldn't see me. They were completely oblivious to my presence, and were totally immersed in the world I had just left. They were desperately trying to bring "me" back.

As I recall the experience, again the closest comparison I can put into words is, that it was very much like being at the movies. You've been to the movies -- you know what it's like. As you sit there watching all the action, you probably give little or no thought to the Projectionist. The Projectionist makes all the action possible. In my new world I was very much aware of the projectionist. I couldn't see Him -- but I know He was there. Before the movie starts, the man in the booth switches on the light. Without the shaft of light, nothing is visible, nothing exists. In my new environment, I came to the instant realization that "I" was the Light. "I" was the necessary ingredient that made all the moving "pictures" possible.

The picture of my body lying there on the bed had no movement in it. The light was missing. It had been snapped off by the Projectionist way up there in the "booth".

More on this later.

I "Found" The Light

When you die, it's my best feeling the same thing will happen to you. The light will go out, you'll leave your body, and for a moment if you look, you'll still see it lying there. Then with a final glance, you will leave it for ever. Your need for a physical body has ended -- but a body of a different kind is ready and waiting for you.

Why You Leave Your Body

I learned that leaving the body is the perfectly natural thing to do. It's old, it's worn out, it's been involved in an "accident", or the "lease" has run out.

Another cause of "death" - is "disease".

"Dis-ease" is exactly what the word implies. "You" are not at "ease" in your "house". So ---- you move out.

"Where do you go?" You go back to the place where you came from before you moved in. You go to where "God" is. This is the same place from which you originated. Some people call it the "body of Christ".

If by "Christ" they mean "light", then the word is an exact one, and is interchangeable with "God".

Later on I'll share more with you about "Christ", and still more about "God."

However, at this point, let me make a comparison, even if it is a little repetitious.

If the house you lived in - in the world you "know", had deteriorated so badly that the roof continually leaked, or the foundations were crumbling, or the walls were collapsing, you'd move out as quickly as possible.

If your house was sound, but a sudden annihilating accident occurred and ripped it apart, you'd still vacate it at the first opportunity. Then having moved out -- but still needing a place to live, you'd retreat to an area of safety until another house was ready for you to "occupy."

In essence, that's what happens when you "die". You simply move out. When a new and suitable house becomes available, you move in and continue your life from where it left off.

Some of my older readers will recall the old silent movie era when the drama we were watching was presented to us in exciting "episodes".

At the end of episode one, we'd leave the theater with the hero hanging on to a branch of a tree, which in turn was growing at the edge of a precipice. The branch was breaking under his weight, and his death was inevitable. The last scene as the episode concluded, was a "close up" of the jagged rocks, the raging river far below, and a return shot of the horror struck eyes of the hero.

The projectionist in the booth had come to the end of that particular "reel", and the message on the screen would say -- "To be continued, watch for, and don't miss next week's exciting episode."

As "corny" as these comparisons are, they do depict in simple form the exact analogy between one "episode" of our "life" and the next.

I will deal with more of these comparisons in a later chapter. They have far more relevance than it first appears.

As a matter of fact, I truly believe it would be more helpful to your total understanding, if at this stage, you regarded yourself as exactly what you indeed are. "You" are a necessary and most important "actor" in the continuing and unfolding drama we refer to as "life".

As Shakespeare so aptly put it in <u>As You Like It</u>:

> "All the world's a stage,
> And all the men and women merely players.
> They have their exits and their entrances;
> And one man in his time - plays many parts."

The PLAYWRIGHT has written the play. YOU have a part in it --, and only YOU can play that part. Of course, as in any play, you are not on stage ALL the time. Other players in the cast are playing their parts, and at times you are in the "wings" waiting for your "cue" to rejoin the cast.

When there is another part for you to play, you'll be "called". There is absolutely no need to get over anxious, and you shouldn't try to play any parts that were not written for you. As they say in show biz, - "Don't call Him--He'll call you".

Meanwhile, the show must go on, and the drama continued. If all you've had so far is a "bit part", study your role and discover its deeper significance. As you prove your ability to play a larger part based upon your understanding of the entire script, the opportunity will be presented to you to do so.

Death is not the final curtain, it's merely an intermission between "acts".

The Revelation

Again and repetitiously, the most significant discovery I made after my "death" was that "I" -- the real "me"-- was not my body. For those of you who on the surface acknowledge a similar belief, be sure you are not in a subtle way, still living your life as though you _are_ your body.

Unless you daily and constantly remind yourself who you really are, the vague recognition that "you" are eternal -- and your body only temporary, will not demonstrate your "immortality" in your day to day "here and now" life.

When your body grows old, tired, decrepit, or diseased, and "dies", "you" do not die with it. "You" never become old, tired, decrepit or diseased. "You" never "die".

When you move out of your body in so called "death",-- "you" will be free from the limitations and confinement of your temporary residence, and be ready for the next phase of your eternal life.

If, while playing your current role, you probe into the "mysteries" of the "big picture", and became further "enlightened", your next "part" will be a larger one.

Chapter Three

GENESIS

<u>Where And How "You" Began</u>

All of us live in a world we try to explain with
"words". However, we must always remember that the words
are not the things we are trying to explain or describe.
The word labels we attach to seemingly separate "parts"
of our life, are not the parts of our life in themselves.
They are merely labels and nothing else. In and of themselves, they have no power to "cure" or "regenerate" us,
than do the labels attached to the prescriptions we get
from the pharmacist.

In the language we use to communicate in "this"
world, we say you must be "born" before you can "die".
Using other words, to explain the same thing, we say you
must have a beginning before you can have an end.

All these "words" however, have no truth in "reality".
They do serve a purpose in identifying what appears to
be differentiated "parts", but they also cloud and hide
the truth.

The words we use are the language of our "senses".
When you use these words it's your senses that tell you
to use them. Your senses are "part" of your body, and
since your body isn't you, it doesn't tell you the truth.

Remember, "you" tell your body what to do, your body doesn't tell you. As long as you allow your body senses to tell you what to do and what to believe, you are not getting the truth. The house you live in doesn't tell you what color to paint the trim, or how to decorate the interior. You tell the house.

Don't listen to what your body senses tell you. Your body is a liar, and the truth isn't in it.

"You Are Eternal"

Your body senses will tell you that you <u>do</u> have a beginning -- and an end. The real truth is, it's your body that has a beginning and an end ---- not "you".

Your body is the all time great deceiver. It makes a great deal of noise and, if you listen to it -- you'll be deceived. What you should do is listen to the "silence" of your "self". To do this, you must say with "Christ", "get thee behind me Satan." Then listen to your "father" which is within you, for your "father" and "you" are ONE.

As that small child said to me, "Are you sure you grown ups <u>really</u> know what you are doing?"

Your Body Is Temporary

Your body and your body senses can't possibly tell you the truth about something of which they have no know-ledge. Their existence as body and body senses is only temporary. It's no wonder, then, that the story they tell you is the temporary and constantly changing part of your life, and not the eternal or the "real thing". When I "died" I learned the "whole" story, not just that portion of it my body had been telling me about.

Since the world in which we now live, the temporary world of the body and the senses, uses "words" to transmit thoughts and explain and describe experiences, I will have to use words to describe and share with you the so-called processes of "life" and "death", and our apparent "beginnings and endings".

I ask you, however, to listen to the silences between the words -, that's where you will find the truth. The silence is where "you" are, the words and the sound of the words is where your body is. "Be still -- and know that "I" am there".

The Cosmic Imagination

"You" began in your earthly father's "imagination" in the same way the world you live in began in your "spiritual" father's imagination.

Special Note

The next thought I will share with you contains the most significant "words" in the entire book. I suggest you read them slowly and study them carefully. Then be quiet and very "still". The silence will give you the key which will unlock the "real" meaning of every "word" that follows.

While I was "dead", I discovered that . . .

THE IMAGINATION IS THE PLACE WHERE ALL THINGS HAVE THEIR BEGINNING

This includes you, me, every other "thing" in the world, and the world and the universe itself.

I said THE IMAGINATION, to emphasize there is only ONE imagination. This ONE imagination is seemingly divided into two (including "yours") and many more if you include every- one who seemingly possesses an imagination.

However, "your" imagination, as well as mine, is in an exact sense, just a "part" of the total and universal imag- ination. I learned that the immensity and all pervasiveness of the Cosmic Imagination our Creator used to create us and the world we "live" in, is ours to use for the asking.

Didn't He say "Ask and ye shall receive---knock and it shall be opened unto you?"

As co-creators with the Creator who created us, we are limited in the scope of our creations only by the meager or major way we use the Cosmic Imagination He has made available to us.

Just Imagine ------

"You" can share the same imagination your creator
used to IMAGE and create the world, to create the kind
of world YOU have imagined and imaged!

The IMAGINATION is a "place" filled with embryonic
"images".

"God" said, (more about God later) "Let us make man
in our own "IMAGE". (Genesis Chapter 1 Verse 26, in the
Book of Instructions) "You" were "imaged" into being in
exactly the same way the "world" was imaged into being.
These images were "developed" from the huge storehouse
of images in THE COSMIC IMAGINATION. God holds the key
to this storehouse, and will open it up anytime you "ask".

"God" was your creator. "You" were created in HIS
image. He imaged and imagined you into being in the
same way He imaged and imagined everything else into being.

Every "thing" that is "born", exists before it is
born, in THE IMAGINATION. When it is born or brought into
existence, it becomes "visible" to the "senses". Prior
to that, it exists as an image in the imagination, and
is invisible to the senses. "God" used His imagination to
bring you into existence. He imaged exactly what you would
look like when visible, "formed" a perfect image, and
poured "you" into the "form".

While you were "formless" and invisible, all was dark
and void. Then "God" said -- "Let there be Light" -- and

there was light. The creation of light was the start of the creation of "you". You are Light, and the light that is within you will light up your body (house) until the light goes out. Then all will be "dark and void". You, the Light, will return to your Eternal Home, "THE IMAGINATION" until you are called upon once more to light up another "body".

Benjamin Franklin knew what this was all about when he gave instructions for the following words to be etched on his tombstone.

Here Lies

The "Body" of Benjamin Franklin

Printer,

Like the Cover of an Old Book

Its Contents Torn Out

and

Stripped of its Lettering

and Gilding,

Food for the Worms ---

But the "Work" shall not be Lost,

For it Will as He Believed,

Appear Once More

In a New and More Elegant Edition

- Revised and Corrected by the Author

He knew whereof he spoke. I learned this same truth while I was "dead". HIS-tory has recorded that a great deal of Light shone upon the world from this great man. Benjamin Franklin's earthly life exemplified the "words", "Let your light shine before you".

What man has done --- other men can do. Once you know that "you" are "Light" and you can have as much Light as you ask for, your Light will shine more brightly before you.

You Were Made In The

"Image" of God

Every "thing" exists in the imagination before it exists in what we call "reality".

The telephone did not exist in reality until 1876, but its inventor, Alexander Graham Bell, "imaged" it long before that in his imagination. In actual fact of course, the telephone had always existed. It was stored, invisible to the "senses" in THE IMAGINATION. Bell "asked" for it, imaged it, and when the image "appeared" to him, he brought it into "visible" existence.

The image comes first, then comes the "thing" imaged. No "thing" can be brought into existence unless it is imaged and imagined first.

Remember,

"The Imagination is the Place Where All Things Have
Their Beginning"

What I have shared with you, not only tells you how you got here, but how "everything" got here.

It also tells you "what" you are.

In the next chapter, I will go into this phase of your "being" with you exactly as it was given to me.

I didn't know these things until I "died". However, during that brief period of time I spent away from my body, I _did_ discover what I was made of -- and what you are made of too.

I'll also explain "God" to you as He explained Himself to me.

Chapter Four

NEVER LIE TO A CHILD -------

Before I died on that fateful morning of December 16, I hadn't been a particularly religious man. I had never been a member of any denominational church, although being an Englishman, I was a nominal Episcopalian.

During my life, I had attended services at both Protestant and Catholic churches. As a child I attended Sunday School, and had earned a book full of golden stars for regular attendance.

As an impressionable youngster, it was there my ideas about church, Christianity, and the teachers and teachings about religion were formed. The memories and impressions of those early years in Sunday School are vivid ones. I remember them in all their clarity to this day.

As a result of my "dying" experiences and my confused beliefs before this event, I am convinced these teachings were all "fairy tales".

Even in my childhood days, I couldn't believe a word they taught me. But I desperately WANTED to believe.

Those early feelings of puzzled non-belief were nurtured within me by ministers of the cloth and by lay Sunday School teachers alike.

The word pictures painted in my mind as a child by

my religious mentors were totally unbelievable. The
answers they gave to my sincere and innocent questions
had an incredible ring of untruth about them. My
earnest young soul cried out in agony for the truth.

I asked for bread, and they fed me stones.

Here in essence, is a summary of what they told me.

God was a man. An old man. He had a long, white
beard. He sat on a throne, like a King, high up in the
clouds. He was surrounded by "angels" who were flying
around Him with diaphanous, fluttering wings. On His
white gowned lap was a huge book, open in the middle, and
into which He entered and recorded any and all misdeeds I
committed.

Although He had a kind, fatherly face, He was always
watching me. Every sin I had committed would be presented
as evidence of my wicked life on "Judgement Day".

Frankly, I could never make up my mind whether my
religious tutors believed these stories themselves, or
whether they thought I was so ignorant and limited in my
capacity to understand, that they told me these stories
to scare me.

As a result, my hunger for the truth was never satis-
fied, and my thirst for the meaning of life was never
quenched. Well meaning as these "fairy tales" might
have been, they were disastrous to my innocent quest for
the truth.

First of all, no matter how desperately I tried, I just couldn't bring myself to believe that "God" was a man.

Even a Super Man.

Back in those days, decades before women's "lib", I thought these stories were grossly unfair to women. Especially in view of my observations that women were eminently more God-like than men.

It was the men who were killing and maiming other men in wars around the world. It was the women who were binding the wounds.

By their "words" they taught me that God said "Love ye one another". In their lives they taught me how men should kill one another. During the "Great War", the British claimed God was on their side. The Germans declared He was on theirs. As a youngster, I was not blind to these obvious anomalies. They wounded my inate sense of honesty, and undermined my feelings of trust in my "elders".

Failing to get the truth from my peers, I neverthe-less vowed I would learn the truth -- even if it killed me.

And I did -- and it did.

At this period of my life, I was hungry for the truth. I desperately wanted to KNOW God and discover the answers to all the seeming mysteries surrounding Him.

I was frustrated and hurt by the never ending succession of evasions and "fairy tales". I was even more bewildered by the sincere but unbelievably conflicting "explanations" I received.

Deep down inside I ached for something in which I could "believe". It seemed as though every minister and Sunday School teacher had different answers for the same simple questions.

However, they all agreed on one thing.

There was a "heaven" and there was a "hell".

Heaven was the place where God was, and Hell was the place where the Devil was. If you were good, you went to Heaven; if you were bad, you went to Hell. They also told me the fortunate ones who went to Heaven would find peace, and all would be bright and beautiful. If you went to Hell, you'd burn in a lake of fire for all eternity. Without all the "trimmings", this was the unilateral, definitive Christian teaching I received as a child.

As A Child .....

I rejected it lock, stock and barrel. To me, it all seemed utterly barbarous. The God I felt existed (and I had absolutely no doubt in my mind that God DID exist) was not the kind of God who would sentence "sinners" to such a _devilish_ fate.

I rejected the entire concoction as nothing more than the distorted fantasies of sincere individuals who, although they had no conception of the truth themselves, were teaching others what somebody else had taught them.

I concluded, even at that early age, it was a case of the blind leading the blind.

My innocent sense of "fairness" just would not allow me to believe that a just God, a God who had gone to such lengths to "make" me, would then destroy me by throwing me physically into a lake of burning fire.

It also told me that, since I didn't know all the "rules of the game", I would be given as much time as I needed to learn them. My conscience told me that if I were God, I wouldn't do this kind of thing to my worst enemy.

As a youngster, something inside me whispered that God loved me, and had given me a mind to reason things out. It was only one of the gifts He had given me, but I was to use it to the very best of my ability.

None of these teachings were reasonable. It was the most unbalanced and ill conceived story I had ever heard. I rejected the whole thing as preposterous and totally unbelievable, but never gave up my search for the truth. I asked God to show me the truth a thousand times. In His own "time", He did, in a strange and wonderful way.

I will continue to share it with you in the ensuing chapters of this book. I touch on the early years of my life -- because it may remind you of yours.

Flash Back

While I was "dead", my entire life flashed before me. It was just like an authentic replay of one of those "This is Your Life" television series. And, just like the series, I'll also share with you a few of the "flashbacks".

Of course, none of these comparisons are precise. The "This is Your Life" television show lasted a full half hour. I seemed to re-live my whole life in but the "twinkling of an eye".

After my experience of "dying", I would like to make a suggestion or two.

First, if you don't know the truth yourself, tell the "child" the truth and <u>say</u> you don't "know".

Second, take the child's hand gently in yours and discover the truth together. Never, never lie to a child.

Remember, in the Book of Instruction, it says

"and a little child shall lead them".

Shouldn't we grown-ups ask OURSELVES

"Do we really know what we are doing?"

Chapter Five

ALPHA AND OMEGA

And God said

"Let there be Light, and there was Light".
When I died and left my body, I immediately went to where
God was. Later, when I was interviewed by Virginia Gabriele of the Daily Press, she informed me that the
account I gave her of my journey into the "beyond", was
remarkably similar to other reports she had read con-
cerning other people who had "died" and "come back".

They all told of travelling through a long, dark
tunnel, and then emerging into an indescribable "white
light".

My experience was almost the same, except the ines-
capable realization came to me -- that "I" was an integral
part of that indescribable white light. I was also aware
that God was with me, just as He was when He said

"Let there be Light'

I didn't hear any "words". The realization of the
truth and the answers to my questions of a lifetime
became part of my consciousness in the twinkling of an
eye.

In that timeless journey into darkness and light,
the truth I so desperately wanted to discover as a child

was revealed to me in a sudden blaze of instant "knowing".

I was no longer listening to the theories and fantasies of people who hadn't "been there". I saw the truth exactly as it is written in God's Book of Instructions.

No longer was I listening to more and more about less and less. The information I received was impressed upon my consciousness with the majesty and authority that only truth can convey.

Deep down inside all of us is something I like to describe as a tiny, delicate "bell". When the truth strikes it -- it reverberates with the unmistakable ring of truth. It's a sound that is beyond counterfeiting. Each one of us knows that sound when we hear it. It's a silent sound. The silence from which truth emerges from the "darkness" into the "light".

There are hundreds, and maybe thousands of different interpretations as to what the "words" in the Bible mean.

Wars have been fought and millions have been killed to decide which interpretation was "right".

In spite of that, I am convinced that this same Bible-- the book I call the Book of Instructions, does indeed give us the answers to all our questions. It repeatedly tells us to "seek the light".

As a result of my "out of the body" experiences, I decided to read these instructions again. I wanted to "match" them against what had been revealed to me while I was "dead".

No longer was it necessary for me to "believe" what others ---- less "experienced" than myself had to say. They had never "been there". I had been where the buried treasure was, had come back with a map, and could lead others to where the treasure was "buried". This book is not just another interpretation -- or the beginning of another "denomination". Neither does it seek to "proselyte".

It's simply an "eye" witness account of what happens when you "DIE", a description of where you "go", and in my case -- what it's like to "come back".

I was told to check the Book of Instructions. I was told where to check. I was told to refer to it as the Book of Instructions.

I Learned That ------

The world "here" is patterned after the world "there". The world I so briefly visited. Everything God makes comes with an instruction book. Everything man makes comes with an instruction book.

An instruction book tells us how a given item is "put together". It tells us what its purpose is -- and how to maintain it. It explains how to fix it when it goes wrong, gives us an itemized list of its "parts", and comes with a written guarantee. It also bears the name or logo of the manufacturer. The guarantee stipulates that if it doesn't work satisfactorily, it can be returned and replaced with a "new" one.

There's more of course, but in essence, this is

what the Bible, our Book of Instructions tells us too.

Since man can create only that which he already has

within himself, it's no surprise that man, like God,

furnished an instruction book with his creations. Man's

book of instructions and guarantee can't be compared

with what God supplies, but it is a reasonable facsimile.

Man's instructions are imperfect, and his guarantee is

limited. God's instructions are perfect, and His guarantee

is for ever. Let's take a look at God's Book of Instruc-

tions, see what it says, then relate it to what I learned

during my visit to the place where "everything begins".

In The Beginning

"In the beginning, God created the Heaven and the

Earth". (two opposites)

And the "earth" was without form and void, and dark-

ness was upon the face of the deep. And God said, 'let

there be light'. And God saw the light that it was good,

and God divided the light from the darkness".

I found God -- where He said He was ---- in the dark-

ness of that long, black tunnel, or "void". "He expressed

Himself to me as an "indescribable white light". He was

in Truth, the Light at the end of the tunnel.

God made all things. The Book of Instructions tells

us that "All things were made by Him, and without Him

not anything was made".

God made everything out of "Himself". The first "thing" He made was "light". Everything that is made, is made of Light. Jesus, the "Christ" came to show us that "Light".

When I died, I found this to be perfectly true. It was while I was "dead" and had returned to my Maker, to the place where everything is made, that I discovered that "Christ" -- the Light of the world -- WAS IN ME!

In the beginning -- "all was dark and void". This too was clearly revealed to me. This was the long, dark, tunnel I travelled through to eventually "find" the Light. (As did many others who have made the same journey and reported the same experience). When I emerged to the "light" it truly was indescribable, and filled with "peace and joy".

This indeed was "Heaven". This was the place where we are all transformed into "light". I felt supremely happy and contented. I felt I had returned "home". It was there I discovered "I" was light, and that "Christ" and the "Light" are one. It was this light that illuminated the darkness.

Darkness becomes illuminated and filled with light, in the same way Silence is filled with Sound. First, there is Darkness, non-motion, then there is light -- MOTION. First there is Silence, non-motion, then there is Sound ---- MOTION.

I found it all there in the Book of Instructions.

"In the beginning was the 'Word', and the 'Word' was God" The "Word" was the way God expressed Himself and made Himself apparent and visible to man. Before there was the word -- there was silence. There always is-- isn't there?

Silence is the father of Sound in the same way God is the Father of Light. The process is identical.

Silence contains, and IS Sound, in the same way God contains, and IS LIGHT.

Sound is in silence, and silence begets sound. Light is in God -- and God begets Light. The child is in the father and the father begets the child.

Christ, "The Light of the World" was God's only begotten Son. Light is the physical manifestation of God. "Christ" was also the physical manifestation of God in the "flesh". God's first "production" was Light. Then in conformity with God's law of production, (every-thing after its own kind), Light begat everything else. God is the "Father", the Light, (Christ) His only begot-ten son. The Light is the primeval "stuff" of which we are all made. Christ, the Light, is in all of us, and by that relationship we are all "sons" of God. We are all direct descendants of the ONE FATHER who made us all of the same original "stuff".

This is the way it's recorded in the Book of Instructions, and this is the way I found it to be.

However, the "Words" are not the things they describe or explain. Don't get caught up in the "words".

Your dictionary will tell you in words, that light travels at a speed of 186,400 miles per second. If you believe that -- have you ever asked yourself at what speed darkness travels? Darkness has no "speed". Darkness is non-motion. Darkness is also described as the "absence" of light, but darkness is no more the absence of light than Silence is the absence of sound. Sound comes from silence in the same way Light comes from darkness.

Darkness begets Light. Silence begets Sound. When you go into the silence and darkness of your imagination to "form" an "idea", you instantly know you've "got it" when the "light" goes on. When there is something you don't "know", you are in the "dark" until some "light" is thrown on the "matter". Then what was un-known becomes known. What was invisible becomes visible. You can "see" it all now.

It's exactly the same with "knowing" and "seeing" God. Once you know where God is -- you can go to "Him". God is in that silent and invisible part of your being you call your imagination. He is unknown to you until you go there and find Him. It has been said, that if God didn't exist -- someone would have to imagine Him. Your imagination is a real place. You "know" that. You use it every day. You

will find everything you could possibly need there.
The imagination is the storehouse of all "things". When
you ask -- you receive. When you knock, the door is
opened. The POWER of your imagination is GOD.
THE IMAGINATION IS THE PLACE WHERE ALL THINGS HAVE THEIR
BEGINNING.

You'll find God right in your imagination. God is
your imagination. He is ALL things and the Creator of
ALL things.

"In the Beginning God Created------------"

Your imagination is not only the place where all things
have their beginning --- IT IS THE BEGINNING.

When you go into your imagination to find the answers
to your questions, you are going to the right place. You
are going directly to God.

God is where all things are created -- in the imagination. Nothing which was ever created was not IMAGE --ined
first, God is ALL. You go to God when you want something --
anything -- everything, because that's where "every-thing"
is. You must know where God lives, moves and has His
being. He lives, moves, and has His being in the imagination -- where all things move, live, and have their being.

Before you "knock"--all is dark and void. Before you

"ask" -- all is dark and void. But that's where all the answers are. That's where all the power is. When you knock and ask, ---- you switch on the power, and immediately ---- the light goes on.

The atheist who says he doesn't believe in God uses that very same power -- which is God, to come to the conscious decision there is no God. Without that power, the existence of which he denies, he would have no consciousness, and could not make a conscious decision. The power he uses to say there is no God ------- IS GOD.

"God" is a "word". In itself as a word, it has no power. In exactly the same sense, the word "atom" has no power.

The power is in that which the word describes or explains. To the naked senses the atom is unobservable. It is silent. The "power" only expresses itself to the senses when it becomes MOTION. The power of the atom is expressed as an indescribable white light. The power of God is expressed as an indescribable white light.

The difference is in magnitude. God is the GREAT LIGHT. The atom is the LESSER LIGHT. The atom expresses the presence and the power of God microcosmically. "Christ" expresses the presence and the power of God macrocosmically.

However diminished and microcosmic our LIGHT is, --- to the extent that we have it -- we express it as the presence of Christ and the Power of God.

God is the word "cause" which powers your imagination ---- the place where all things have their beginning. The "effects" are the images you imagine in your imagination.

In The Beginning ------- God

At this point, I would like to quote from the Book of Instructions. The following comes from St. John, Chapter 1 verses 1-9.

> "In the beginning was the Word, and the Word
> was with God, and the Word <u>was</u> God
> The same was in the beginning with God.
> All things were made by him; and without
> Him was not anything made that was made.
> In Him was life; <u>and the life was the light
> of men</u>.
> And the light shineth in the darkness;
> and the darkness comprehended it not.
> There was a man sent from God whose name was John.
> The same came for a witness, to bear witness
>   of the Light, that all men through him
>   might believe.
> He was not that Light, but was sent to bear
>   witness of that Light.
> <u>That</u> was the true Light, which lighteth every
>   man that cometh into the world."

While I was in the other world, I was "told" to read these specific verses. --- I was also "told" to read "The Sermon on the Mount". I believe the above verses express what I have attempted to express, only much more clearly.

Note especially the upper and lower class treatment of the word "light". It represents the Greater and the Lesser Light.

Chapter Six

WE LIVE IN TWO WORLDS

Not a single word was spoken while I was in the "other" world. Yet everything I am sharing with you "here", I learned from the "sound" of a silent voice "there".

Before I "died", I knew none of these things. While I was dead, I came to know them all.

During that timeless interval when I visited the creative workshop where "all things are made", I learned all I have already shared with you, and experienced everything I am about to share.

The time I spent at the center of God's expanding universe was infinitesmal by "this" world's standards, but it was all Eternity when measured by the sidereal chronology of the "other" world.

"A thousand years shall be but as a single day".

It was there I was given the answers to the "myst-eries" of the two worlds we all live in. I was also shown the way to live in these two worlds.

In "this world, the world of the senses, the world we "live" in, before we go to the world we "die" in, we have developed an ever expanding lexicon of "words" to label, describe and explain its existence.

However, they are merely the communication tools of the IMAGINEER who uses them to support and give seeming substance to his imagined images.

Please permit me the use of a paradigm, while you go into the silence of your being for the answer.

Merely use my example to reverse yourself from your motion and noise filled senses, into the stillness and silence of your IMAGINATION.

The Duality of Our Being

Already in this book, we have delved into the domain of dualism. We have talked about "this" world and the "other" world. We have also talked about the "sense" world and the "spirit" world. We have explored the seeming extremities of "life" and "death". This kind of word supported imagery makes us as mortals -- either happy or unhappy. Like all things of the senses, it expresses itself as "opposites". It makes us optimistic or pessimistic. Positive or negative. It gives us pleasure or pain, and fills us with either joy or despair.

All these "emotions" are seemingly dualistic opposites of the ONE same thing.

We are, on the one hand, temporarily titillated by the pleasing immediacy of movement, emotion, and motion they provide, and then at almost the same time it seems, we

are shocked and saddened by the sensing and certitude
of their inevitable "end". Making love is something you
might want to last forever. But you "know" that at the
very climax of your ecstasy will come the anticlimatic
reality of its all too temporary existence.

All sense related "realities" are convincingly seeming
dualities. They are, at one and the same time, two "opposites" of the same thing.

We talk about day -- and know it is becoming night.
We refer to that which lives, and yet we know it will die.
When we are young, we know we are becoming old. This
very knowing is the TRUTH we hide from ourselves by using
words to divide one thing into two. God (good),the Devil
(evil).

I Find The "One"

With the speed of light in the darkness of the
other world, I learned there is only ONE.

This One who we know as God, IMAGES, and then REFLECTS
the "sensed" many. When we see the "reflection" of our
ONE self in the placid stillness of a limpid pool, we
sense there is TWO. When we see the reflection of
God's expression of Him-self we also sense two.

I learned there is only ONE.

There is no such thing as Life and Death. There is
only LIFE -- and that is Life Eternal.

Just as we sleep between one day and the next, so we "sleep" between one life and the next.

There is no UP, and there is no DOWN. When the astronauts were on the Earth, they looked up at the moon. When they were on the moon, they didn't look down at the earth. They still looked UP, and the earth was now where the moon "was". As long as we continue to look "out there", we will continue to see only those things we can "sense".

It is not until we look "in here" that we will know what those things "out there" really are.

They are nothing more than our projected images reflected back to us from the limitless reflective screen of "space". They are creations or productions of our imagination in the same way that the movie we watch is the creation and production of the movie producer's imagination.

THERE IS ONLY ONE

There is only ONE, seemingly divided (or multiplied) into many. These untold billions of created unit "parts" owe their "being" to our sensed recognition of their light-fast moving ---- and seemingly separated existence.

Every "thing" began with the ONE -- imaging motion, and thereby becoming its polarized, divided self image.

This is how darkness became light.

"And the earth was without form and void;
and darkness was upon the face of the deep.
And the "spirit" of God MOVED upon the face
of the water, and God said LET THERE BE LIGHT
-----------AND THERE WAS LIGHT.

This is how stillness becomes "motion", how Silence becomes Sound, and how "formlessness" becomes "form".

"And the earth was without form and void".

The first "image" was "motion", and motion produces "motion pictures".

These pictures are the pictures we see with our senses. They are not "real". When we go to the "movies", what we are really watching is a series of "stills" or separate "shots" joined together by fast motion making a "motion picture". But the motion pictures we see, are not the real live "actors" who play in those pictures and whose "actions" are reflected back to us from the silver screen.

Our senses deceive us. They never tell us the TRUTH. In point of fact, we go to the movies to be <u>deceived</u>.

We know it isn't "real" and we know it isn't true. God first imaged "motion" and this motion is what we call "light". You don't "see" the motion, you see the sensed result of this motion -- which <u>is</u> LIGHT.

Motion and Light is One, but it seems like Two to the senses. They are the polarized, seemingly separated and opposite attributes of the ONE thing, that which we call "God".

IS <u>THIS</u> WORLD REAL?

In the sense world it's the "REAL THING". While we
live, move, and have our being in this sensed, mortal
and temporary house we call our body it is indeed one
of the worlds in which we live our dual existence.

This "double" life is the "cause" of all our "effects".
As long as we sense these two worlds, we are living what
is said to be a "normal" existence. However, some of us
in our more troubled states, where a complete or partial
disintegration of the relative simplicity of dualism has
been fragmented into multisensed lives, are said to be
suffering from "schizophrenia". This is another "word"
which is by no means that which it describes.

What has happened here, is our normal dualistic per-
ception or sensing has been split or multiplied into
imaged mutations of the simple two way conceptions we
can handle with "ease". This is one form of dis-ease, but
in order that my readers do not get schizophrenic at this
point, I will confine the seeming multi-units of the ONE
into its normal sensed division of two. From this basic
beginning, we can expand our comprehension into the next
concept ---- the "Trinity".

"MY FATHER AND I ARE ONE"

You are just like God. God made you in His image.
God made you from Himself. God is a part of you. That part

of you which is God, is the power plant which powers your life. All power resides in and comes from God. When He imaged you, a part of His power gave life to that image. The God power within you enables you to be a co-creator with God. He creates His creations with His Cosmic power. You create your creations with that share of His Cosmic power with which He endowed you at birth.

Just as God expands and "multiplies" His power -- you can expand and "multiply" your power. More on this later.

God is the observer of His creations. You are the observer of your creations. You are the creator and ob-server of your children. God is the creator and observer of His children. Like God, you create TWO in your imag-ination by the very act of "imaging", and like God, you remain still and motionless as the IMAGINEER and OBSERVER or your creation. Your creation is TWO. You and your imaged creation is TWO -- and the materialized and vis-ible result of your imaged creation is THREE -- the TRINITY of "being".

The Book of Instructions tells it this way.

"So God created man in His own image. In the image of God created He him, male and female He created them."

This is the created and completed TRINITY. It appears in GENESIS (The Beginning) Chapter 1, verse 27.

If the "word" explanation in the Book of Instructions doesn't make sense, or your sensed awareness of its meaning seems confused, don't worry about it at this point. As we proceed, it will all become clear.

In the same way that every "thing" you create issues from your imagination, and is therefore a part of you, so indeed are you a part of it.

In fact, you center it and control it. You are the central "seed" from which it will grow.

Just as God resides and lives in you as one of His children -- one of His creations, so you reside and live in your children -- which are your creations.

Your children are your creations. Without THAT part of you which you implanted within them -- your "seed", your "blood", they would not and could not "exist".

God's children are His creations. Without the seed He implanted in you and the "power" of His "blood", you would not and could not "exist".

If this all seems rather mysterious and miraculous, it is if you try to BELIEVE with the sensed "effects" of the created part of you instead of the spiritual "cause" of the CREATIVE part of you.

It was the Christ Jesus who explained His "miracles" by saying "It is not I that doeth these things --- it's the Father which is within me."

He further amazed His listeners when He added "And

as great as these things are that I do, -- even greater
things than these will ye do."

There was nothing mysterious or ambiguous about His
explanation. Christ knew, and I learned, that man can
only do in miniature what God can do in magnitude.

Within the framework that Christ exemplified by
His actions, there is nothing impossible of "conceiving"
and "achieving". Just go to your imagination -- where the
Father is, image what you can conceive and you will
achieve.

Christ healed the sick and raised the dead, but
it was the FATHER WITHIN THAT DID THESE THINGS.

The Father (the power) is within us -- and it is the
Father -- which is the power that doeth these things.
"Know ye not that ye are the temple of the living God?"

The Father is our life source and our power source.
He appears to us in the form of LIGHT. This LIGHT is the
"LIGHT that Lighteth every man that cometh into the world."
This light is the Christ.

There is only ONE, -- God, who by imaging images
makes Himself TWO. He does this by remaining motionless
(like we do when we imagine images) while seemingly dividing
Himself by the motion created by the act of His imagining.

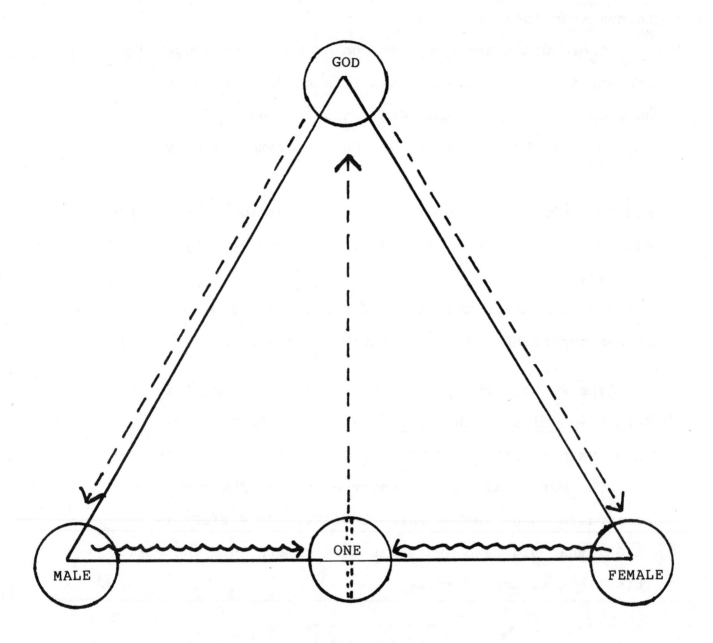

Illustration #1

The "division" between "male" and "female" and the constant and continuing "urge" to get back together to the "ONE" they really are is what we call Love in the spiritual sense and Sex in the physical sense.

In addition to the "word" explanation, I have included in illustration #1 a "symbol-ic" explanation. Symbols came before "words" and are much less complicated.
They appeal less to the senses and more to the imagination.
It has been said that one picture is worth a thousand
"words". This symbol-ic explanation gives a diagrammatic
picture of the motion induced act of self division by
imagined polarization.

But neither words, symbols, or pictures are the
things they try to explain or describe. The builders of
the Great Pyramid at Gizeh tried to tell us this in their
amazingly constructed time capsule. We call it a Pyramid.

They tried to explain the secrets of creation in
mathematical terminology so explicit, that the guarantee
their secrets would fall only into the right hands was
assured by the fact that entirely sensed motivated men
could never understand them. These ingenious safeguards
have protected them to this very day. Isaiah, one of the
contributors to the Book of Instructions said, "And it,
(the PYRAMID) shall be for a sign and for a witness". I
was shown the meaning and the purpose of the Pyramid
during my visit to the "other" world, as it relates to the
system and mathematics of God's miracle of creation. Isn't
it rather surprising that for more than 5,000 years the
advanced technological civilization in which we live has
no agreed upon explanation for its presence, its purpose,

or even how it was built?

A large body of opinion believes it was not built by "men" at all. They say that mere mortals never could have erected such an edifice. At least they add -- not ordinary men as we know them. Pyramid literally means "Fire (or light) in the "Middle", and although the word is not the Pyramid it describes, the word description not only holds the key to the entire mystery of life, but also contains within itself the answers to all the questions mankind has continually asked itself since the dawn of man's emergence on earth.

This enigmatic engineering miracle was imagineered and built as a "sign and a witness" of the way creation comes into being. How the ONE becomes TWO and how the TWO becomes the TRINITY. I was also shown how the re-flected and repetitive process of imaged motion becomes the sensed world we live in, while the "fire" or "Light" is burning on the "altar" in the middle of our body.

Man -- epitomized by the pyramid, and like God, is a silent and motionless observer of His multi-created motion-filled, and seemingly polarized, self images.

"God" and the "Devil"

To our sensed awareness, every "thing" seems to come in TWO'S. They also appear to be opposite to each other. As a matter of fact, we can only explain, describe, or label "things" by comparing them with their opposites.

GOOD and evil

Adam and eve

Heaven and hell

Male and female

North and south

Even the animals went into Noah's ark --- two by two! Each "half" of the duo appears to be related to, but diametrically opposed to the other. In reality, however, they are merely differently sensed aspects of the ONE.

"Our" world, "this" world, would not and could not exist were it not for this seeming opposition and differentiation.

This seeming contrary motion, this ebb and flow of "light waves" of God's invisible imagining is what makes this world "appear" and "felt" by our quintupled sensed body.

Chapter Seven

Cause and Effect

All these seeming opposites are really ONE. They are the sensed effects of the ONE cause.

Joy and despair seem to be opposite emotions, but in reality, they are two faces of the ONE "coin". (Even our coins have a "head" and a "tail".) Joy is the anti-cipation of becoming "happy". Despair is the fear of becoming "unhappy". Very often, one becomes the other when the joy of the "present" becomes the despair of the "future".

Love when "spurned" can become hate, and day becomes night by the mere passage of "time".

All things are always "becoming" something else. They become their "opposites".

The Christian religion could not continue to exist unless there were Sinners and Saints. Good and Evil, Heaven and Hell, and God and the Devil. We try to change the sinner into a saint. We contrast the benefits of Heaven as opposed to the horrors of hell.

If all were saints, and all was heaven, the Christian "work" of changing the damned into the divine would grind to a screeching halt. Its very existence as a "religion" depends entirely upon the continuation of Good and Evil. I learned that the "millenium", the "second coming of Christ," and the "kingdom of Heaven" is "within us".

In the Book of Instructions, the Christ says -- "Know

ye not that the Kingdom of Heaven is WITHIN YOU?" And --
"Ye are the temple of the Living God."

The Pyramid, the "sign and the witness", that which
has the "fire" or light in the "middle" tells us the same
thing. Your fire, your light, is in the "middle" of you.
It is the soul, the seed, the YOU of you. It's the
light that shines on the "altar" in the middle of your
body.

When your light shines so brightly, when your fire
burns so strongly that it "consumes" the "darkness",
which IS the body, the body SENSES, you will become ALL
LIGHT.

At that time, you will "see" the millenium. You will
experience the second coming of the "Christ". You will
enter fully and completely into the Kingdom of Heaven.
You and your Father will be ONE.

IT IS YOUR BODY -- AND YOUR BODY SENSES THAT BLINDS
YOU TO THE REALITY OF THE KINGDOM OF GOD

The Kingdom of God is within you. It's the place
where God is. It's that part of you which is God. As the
Book of Instructions tells us -- "The Kingdom of Heaven
is at hand". It is right there within us -- in the very
center of our being. It IS at hand -- it couldn't possibly be any closer.

From Darkness Into Light

When I became ALL light and no-body, for a brief

moment of "time" I entered into the Kingdom of Heaven.
I was an all consuming light which "fed" on the darkness. As more and more of your "body" is consumed
by the light within you, the body and the body senses
become "less" and the light becomes "greater". The more
"light" you have -- the more truth you "see". I learned
and saw clearly the permanent law of change or "becoming".
Every-thing is always changing into or becoming something else. No-thing disappears.

The new born child is said to be --- beginning to
live --- but it could just as truthfully be said to be
beginning to die. Our "words" are circumscribed and qualified by "time". As "time" changes, our "words" change
too.

The Pyramid represents our body. The fire in the
middle represents our "soul" or our "Light". Inside the
Great Pyramid of Gizeh, are two passages. One is called
the Ascending passage -- and climbs upward toward the
apex. The other is called the Descending passage and
goes downward toward the "pit". Here again are the "two
opposites". The apex is Heaven, the pit, hell.

In the center is the King's Chamber. This represents
the center of your being, the altar upon which your light
burns. It's where God is. It's where your imagination is.

Knowing all this, what possible "good" can it do for
us.

For the answer, let's "back track".

If we know and believe that

"THE IMAGINATION IS THE PLACE WHERE ALL THINGS HAVE THEIR

BEGINNING"

we know where "God" is, where the power is, and where we

must go if we want to "know" God, and share His power.

We also know that our "sensed" world is temporary just as

we know that our body is temporary.

We also know that the "source" of our body and our

body senses is Eternal. We know that "cause" -- is still,

and "effect" is motion. Knowing all this, how do we use

this know-ledge for our temporary and eternal benefit?

We do this by going into the stillness and "cause" --

our imagination, and "image" into being a new creation

or creature of "good" to replace or "change" the old

creation or creature that was "bad".

In short, we become an IMAGINEER -- a new "creat-ure

in Christ". (More on this later). There is no need to

waste "time" and energy trying to destroy "evil" (the

Devil), we merely "repent" (which means to change) and

image "Good" (God).

The Book of Instructions, Matthew 5, verse 39 says,

"But I say unto you -- <u>resist ye not evil</u>".

Look it up and read it yourself.

<u>"Christ" is the Light of Your Life</u>

No-thing is destroyed. It merely changes -- or

becomes something else. It often becomes its "opposite".
This is how the un-saved become "saved" and the "sinner"
becomes a "saint". The unsaved, the "sinner", must "see"
things differently. He must "image" good instead of evil.
When he does this, he "sees" things "differently". The
new "light" within him consumes the darkness (evil),
and he uses it as "fuel" to keep his light burning.

Evil is not destroyed; it's a necessary ingredient
in order to have Good. It is impossible to embrace God
(Good) until you have rejected the Devil (Evil). The
greatest sinners -- "become" the greatest saints.

There is nothing our modern day television evangelists like better than to be able to exhibit and exploit
the most debased and degrading behavior as the "testimony" of a repentant sinner in order to show the world
how he "found Christ". (The Light)

One of the all time favorite "gospel" songs is

"I FOUND THE LIGHT"

The lower the sinner has sunk, the greater his crimes
against himself and society, the higher and louder his
praises and virtues are sung once "he has found the light".

The preacher is almost, but not quite, right when he
implores you to invite "Christ" into your "heart",
accept Him as your personal saviour, -- and "become"
born again. His error, as I discovered when I met "Christ",
is that Christ is already in your "heart". "He is the

Light that Lighteth every man that cometh into the
world!"

Your "heart" is your imagination. It is "dark"
there until you "switch" on the light -- which is Christ.
As soon as you "image" Christ -- or the Light, the darkness "disappears" (think about this "word"), and the
light (Christ) takes its place.

The preacher is really asking you to "image" Christ
instead of the devil. To become "good" instead of "evil,"
But of course he doesn't always put it this simply. The
"babel" of his "words" get in the way, and although
fortunately some people do have a "change of heart", they
seldom know or even suspect what the process is that made
it happen.

As soon as you come to the conscious decision (a
decision for Christ, a decision for the Light, a decision
for "good" instead of "evil") that you want to "change"
from "sinner to saïnt", for the Christ Light to "rule" in
your life instead of the Devil (darkness), you change
your "image" in your imagination (heart) and invite the
new image (Christ, the Light) to come in.

"Resist Ye Not Evil"

I learned there is no need to brood about your old
"self". Don't waste your time and summon up all your
energy to "resist" evil. Don't get locked into a struggle

83

with the same "bad" image you have been imaging for so
long.

Set yourself free by "changing" it into a new image.
You can do this by going into your imagination, and "invite" the Christ image to replace the Devil image. You
image Christ instead of "Satan". In effect, you say "Get
thee behind me Satan", as did the Christ of the Bible.
"YOUR IMAGINATION IS THE PLACE WHERE ALL THINGS HAVE THEIR
BEGINNING."
It's the place where you can set a new course for your
life. If, as a result of the terrible mess you have made
of your life so far, you realize it would take a "miracle"
to change and improve it -- go into your imagination and
"image" one. Your imagination is the place where God is.
It's the place to go when you need a good image to replace
a bad one. Don't worry yourself to death about the past.
You have been merely imaging the "wrong" images. Those
images are stored in your past, but there is no need to
keep taking them out of storage and reflecting them back
to yourself.

Your old images have served their purposes. They are
now "dead". In the Book of Instruction, Christ says --
"Let the dead bury the dead".

If you are happy with the present, don't keep thinking about the past. When you "think", you summon up that
same old unhappy image, and if you continue to look at

the same image that made you unhappy before -- it will be sure to make you unhappy again.

Select the image of your-self and the "future" you want. "Visualize" it until it appears as a perfect picture, and then "produce" the picture.

I'll share with you in the next chapter how this is done -- exactly as it was shared with me.

Play Your Part

Always remind yourself that God, the creator of ALL things, had a blueprint for every "thing" He created before He created it. That blueprint was the "image" He imagined. You must have an "image" too. I was privileged to see the Cosmic Script He has written. He also has provided the stage and the scenery so that you can play your "part". He has arranged the entire production in order that you can play as large a role as you have the imagination, the insight, and the capacity to play.

But that's not all. He has also given you the freedom to DIRECT your own part. The only "directive" He gives you is -- you must follow the script. You are just one of the players in the play -- not the playright. No matter how many times you "flub" your lines, you'll get chance after chance to get them "right". One thing is sure, since there is no understudy to take your place, you'll simply have to go on doing it until you get it right.

Whether you are <u>consciously</u> aware that you are a part of the cast or not, the show must go on. The more consciously aware you are that you <u>do</u> have an important part to play, the more consciously aware you are of the complete "story". It's His-story. During my "death", I was privileged to go to a sneak preview. It was there I became conscious of my part in the drama, and also became privy to the entire script.

The purpose of this book, is to share with you the substance of the "story" and the parts we all must play.

Follow the Script

How long you and I take to "learn our lines" is up to us. However, until our part is played to perfection, we must go on making our entrances and our exits until the drama is over.

If our present part has been poorly played, we must keep on playing it over until we get it right and "see" the "finished" picture as it should be seen.

That's our trouble -- <u>we don't get the picture</u>. Our images are wrong. When we change our image and see the "big" picture, we will be qualified to play a larger role.

We have to be "picture perfect".

"Be ye therefore perfect -- even as your Father which is in Heaven is perfect." (Matthew Chapter 5, verse 48)

For The Best Results --
<u>Do It The Way God Does It</u>

God's creations are perfect originals. Man's creations are imperfect copies of those originals. God endows man with as large a share of His imagination as man desires to make use of. God's creations are reflected on the screen of "space". Man's creations are reflected on the screen of His mental "television" receiver via the medium of space. Man is an incurable and unchangeable "copy cat".

God equips man with a receiving and transmitting apparatus, and man copies this with his "radio".

God supplies man with a "pump" to circulate blood around his body. Man makes a "pump" to circulate fluid around the engine of his car.

God installs a built-in temperature stabiliser in man's body. Man duplicates this with a thermostat in his home.

The human brain is paralleled by the computer, and his eyes are duplicated by the camera.

Man's impressive list of so-called discoveries and "inventions" are merely crudely constructed copies of what God has already provided within man's "body".

The jet plane and automobile cannot operate without an air intake, ignition and exhaust system. Neither can man. Man makes "lesser" copies of himself in order to perpetuate and immortalize himself.

In exactly the same way, God perpetuates and immortalizes Himself through His creation of "man", a potential "lesser" God. Like God, man re-produces and creates everything with a dual nature and purpose. Man's "atomic" power can be used for "good" and "evil". In the Book of Instructions, Isaiah writes of God in Chapter 45, verse 7.

"I form the light, I create darkness,

I create peace and I create evil. I

the Lord do all these things."

That's why there is "bad" in the best of us, and "good" in the worst of us.

Just beneath the surface of our being there is a constant "war" in progress. We reflect that war on the outside of our being with the good and the bad which we do.

In His-story, the slaves will eventually become the masters, and the victors will become the victims.

This "becoming" takes "time", and time is the father that begets the becoming. We have all heard of "Father Time".

With the apparent attributes of good and evil inside each of us, with first one in the "ascendency" and then the other, we live our lives as part time sinners and part time saints. By abortion and by man-made instruments, we shorten the lives of babies who are not yet "born". By still other man-made instruments, we lengthen the lives of the aged who are already "dead". We build a

Cathedral in one block, and a brothel in the next.

How To Put Your World Right

Those of us who persist in imaging what we "think"we

see, instead of imaging what we really want to see, will

continue to do everything in "reverse" and constantly

reflect the negative instead of the positive. We should

develop the best possible picture we can "take" -- not

the worst.

When we look "out there" with our inner camera, we

develop all the bad pictures -- we "see" with our decep-

tive body senses. What we should and MUST do if we want

a "better" world, if we want to be "happy", is the com-

plete opposite.

We must develop good, new images "in here" and then

develop and project them "out there". This knowledge is

the master key that will open up for each one of us the

kind of "self" we so desperately desire, and bring into

"being" the kind of world that is destined to be our Heaven

here on Earth.

We must image the picture of truth, beauty and love

we truly want to "see", and then develop it. We must do

this with our "real" self, our eternal self, that part of

us which is not the sensed body. The "bad" pictures we

see are those reflected back to us by body senses. We

know the body is a liar, and the truth is not in it. As

long as we continue to believe the "body", so long will.

our world continue to be the opposite of what we want
it to be.

In order to change ourselves and the world, we must
"change" our images of our "selves", and "change" our
image of the "world". When we do this, our new, "good"
images will replace the old "bad" images, and the world
"out there" will become the kind of place we really want
"in here".

Remember.

"THE IMAGINATION IS THE PLACE WHERE ALL THINGS HAVE THEIR
BEGINNING"

If you want a new beginning in your life, go to the
place where everything begins. Go to your imagination
and "select" a new image of what you want your life to
be, take a perfect picture of it -- and then develop it.

Stop imaging and developing all those pictures you
don't like, and start imaging and developing pictures you
do like. Then, project the new pictures from "in here" --
"out there".

I was shown that this is the way each of us as individuals can change ourselves and change the world. You
change your "self" by changing your image of yourself.
You change the world by first changing yourself.

Everything in your world begins with you. Everything
begins in your imagination, where you begin and where your
world began.

WHO ARE YOU?

YOU CALL YOUR-SELF -- "I"

When you are conscious of yourself, you call your-self "I". There is only one "I" -- and that's "you". There is only ONE, and there is only one "I".

In the world of mathematics, there is only one number 1. The "number" I emerges from the symbol "0" (Zero). The "I" that is you emerges from the symbol "0" (Zero) when you are "born" and returns to the symbol "0" when you "die". The symbol "0" (Zero) is a similie for the imagination.

In the world you call your world, there is only one "I" and that's you.

When in the Book of Instructions God was asked who He was, He replied "I AM THAT I AM". This simple sentence "tells it all".

The world exists as far as you are concerned only as long as you are in it. You cannot express your "self" unless you refer to yourself as "I".

When you speak about me --you cannot refer to me -- as "I". You cannot refer to any other being in this world as "I". It is "they" or "he" or "her" or "him" or "she" or "you". When I died, "I" no longer existed in this world. "I" had left it and "I" was in the "other" world. This world no longer existed. I was in a new "dimension". From this -- and from my shared experience, you can be sure of one thing. This world, the world you now live in, exists only while you are in it.

When you die, the LIGHT will go out, all will become dark and void, and the world as you "know" it will disappear. It exists only as long as you are in it as a conscious "I". You and I image-ine this world, When we are no longer able to image-ine --- there is no world.

Your world can be just as big and beautiful as your imagination. You share with God, the awesome responsibility of bringing into being anything and everything you can image-ine into being.

My world exists in my imagination. Your world exists in your imagination. As long as you share with God the totality of the cosmic Imagination, you have the fantastic power to bring a whole new world into being. Said in the first person, the "self", you can say, "I have the power to bring the whole new world into being".
Repeat this over and over again to yourself. BELIEVE what you say --- because
"THE IMAGINATION IS THE PLACE WHERE EVERYTHING HAS ITS
BEGINNING"

And God said, "Let us make man in our Image".

Images are made in the Imagination -- Your imagination. The imagination is the ONLY place where images CAN be made. With this kind of God-like awesome power, the sharing with God of His power, you can "change"

your-self to what-ever you can Image-ine yourself to be.
By doing this, you can change the "world" -- your world,
to whatever you want it to be.

WHO ARE YOU?

You are a part of God. God made you out of Himself.
God made you in His IMAGE. You have the same attributes
in a lesser way -- that He has in a greater way. You
are a co-creator with God. God externalizes and immortalizes Himself through His creations. You external-
ize and immortalize yourself through your creations.

JUST IMAGE-INE!!!

YOU COME WITH A GUARANTEE AND AN
INSTRUCTION BOOK

As I write this, it is Christ-mas time. All of us
are familiar with the "knocked down" toys we buy for
our children at this time of the year. They have to be
"put together". They are delivered in a container complete with an Instruction Book which tells us how they are
supposed to work, what their function is, and how to
take care of them.

The first thing we do after opening the packing
case -- is to look for the instruction book. This tells us
how to put all the parts together and make it work as a

complete "whole".

If we attempt to do it ourselves without reading the manufacturer's instructions, we often make a mess of the entire thing. But even when we do read the manual, we often fret and fume and wonder why the instructions aren't written in more simple terms. "Why" we ask ourselves, "doesn't the maker explain the process to us in a language we can understand?"

What I am now sharing with you, is how it was all explained to me in easy to understand words.

It's not meant to be a literary gem, a scholarly work, or an example of the proper way English should be written. In fact, I wish I could communicate to you what was communicated to me without the use of words, because I heard no words. But I did "get the picture".

Many of you may have studied the Bible -- our "In-struction Book", and despaired of ever discovering what it really means. Others listen to the complex and con-fusing interpretations of theologians and religious leaders. Millions more settle for the emotional appeal of tent and television evangelists who ask you to give your heart to "Jesus" and your money to them. In organ-ized Christianity, there are more than five hundred dif-ferent denominations, each one of them claiming their surrogate or personal ability to "save" souls, (through Christ) and each of them claiming "their" way is the "right" way. Amid this babel of voices, it's often a case of the blind leading the blind.'

They tell you where you'll go when you die -- and describe in vivid detail what it will be like when you get there.

But none of them have ever "been there" themselves. They tell you with complete immodesty they are "born again", and with equal immodesty offer to tell you how YOU can be born again. Some question exists in my mind as to whether they really <u>have</u> "seen the LIGHT". When you know that <u>you</u> ARE THE LIGHT -- you can find your own way to "heaven", and you'll never be in the dark again. "The Kingdom of Heaven is Within You". (Book of Instructions)

The untold millions who are afraid of the dark, and who are wandering around like lost "souls", provide a fertile field for exploitation by so-called "soul savers" and others who have made it their <u>business</u> to show you the "way".

The Christ -- the Light said, "I am the way, the truth and the Life". The Christ, the Light within <u>will</u> show you the way. All you need to do is to increase the power of that Light so it will burn a little more brightly, and you will "see" the "way, the truth and the life".

The Masses Are Always Wrong

While I was "out of my body", I was "shown" the utter

futility of "mass" evangelization, and the inevitability of its ultimate collapse as the total and "only" Solution.

This would be occasioned by the flagrant and unconscionable exploitation of their trusting "flocks", and the venality and corruption resulting from the misuses and abuses of their bulging coffers of tithed,* tax free money.

This religious "Watergate" would engulf the "guilty" and the "innocent" soul savers alike.

The edict "Thou shall have no other gods before me" would be trampled under foot in the scramble for "love offerings", "donations", and "partners in Christ" offerings. Money to build "temples" of all kinds and for all purposes would become the new "Gods", and the yardstick by which "success" would be measured would be their "Neilson" ratings, and the number of souls they "saved". There is nothing new under the sun -- and all this, in one form or another, has happened before. But sadly, we seem to learn nothing from "His-story". Although it is said that Jesus "paid" for our sins -- the trusting have "paid" others to put in a "good word" for them ever since.

* Tithing, an excellent principle in itself, is often exploited to unconscionable extremities by greedy, unprincipled charlatans. Avoid the religious huckster----tithe generously as prompted by that quiet, small voice within.

Chapter Eight

FLASHBACK

The Moment of Truth

The instant my heart stopped, I began my journey
into the other world. By earthly time standards, I wasn't
away very long. The nurse who beat on my chest to "bring
me back" said I was only "gone" for a couple of minutes.
It could very well have been only a couple of seconds.
"Time" was not important. Like everything else in this
world, your heart beat consists of two "opposites". There
is the time when it's pumping and the time when it's not
pumping. These two phases of the ONE "pump" are called
systolic and diastolic. The normal time space between the
two is a little less than a second. This time space (O)
is the "zero" from which number one and number two appear.--
Every-thing - all creation, "appears" from no-thing. The
(1) one emerges from the (O) zero in the same way sound
emerges from the "zero" of silence.-This trinity is called
our "life cycle". It lasts about seventy years. However,
as I discovered, this life cycle can be telescoped by
"death" into the miniscule time span of the absence of a
few heart beats. During my expanded zero interval of a
"couple of minutes", my entire life flashed before me.
It was during this time space zero interval, I learned

these things I am sharing with you. I also learned the
real meaning of the "words" in the Book of Instructions.

I have shared some of these with you already.

But first -- the re-run of my life. In my case, it
was just like the "instant replay" we see on television.
I was watching a re-play of my life. There was no screen
title, credits or musical score. It began with startling
suddenness with the very first "frame" -- and flashed
across the screen of my vision -- from birth to death
in the "twinkling of an eye".

But that's not all.

I was also shown the "highlights" of my life. The
times when I increased the totality of my share of the
LIGHT, and the times I diminished it. Some of these
incidents may remind you of similar mis-"takes" in your
life.

I was also "told" that a degree of pre-vision would
be given me in strict ratio to the amount the light in my
life was increased. This "gift" would be presented to
me upon my return to "life". The first one of these pre-
visions -- I experienced, -- something entirely new to
me, was the horrendous tragedy of Toccoa Falls in north
eastern Georgia. This, you may remember, was the Bible
College where a number of students and faculty were
swept away to their "death" by the sudden collapse of the
Toccoa Dam.

Twenty four hours before the disaster occurred, I "saw" it happen in all its pent up fury. I saw the dam shudder, heard the thunderous noise, and then saw the raging torrent sweep down the Falls and wash away everything it met in its path.

With tears in my eyes, I described the scene to my wife. Since I was sleeping in bed at the time I witnessed all these events, we both concluded it must have been a "nightmare". The newspapers and television news the next evening told us otherwise. The disaster had occurred exactly as I had "seen" it.

The next pre-visionary experience also occurred while I was sleeping. This took the form of newspaper headlines. I saw them -- almost as though I had set the type myself. This is exactly what I saw.

CHURCH, OFFICIALS ACCUSED OF MISUSE OF FUNDS*
That was all. No details. No intimation of whether the accusation was justified. Just the headlines. They appeared on "cue" the next day. I was not made aware of which particular church was involved, the precognition of the impending event was most emphatic. An added awareness was the distinct indication that this initial incident would be but a prelude to an even greater event of the same kind.

_____

*The World Wide Church of God (Where the "Father" Herbert Armstrong disavowed and disowned the "Son" - Garner Ted Armstrong)

The "feeling" was impressed upon me that at least one segment of the Christian religion, like politics, was facing its "Watergate"

The third incident I "saw" was a broad view of the Pyramids. I was "told" that this site was to be the location for one of the most historic meetings in modern His-tory.

The "words" impressed upon my consciousness were ---

"I have called my son out of Egypt".

The symbolism accompanying the pre-vision was the sign   ℓ

The scene before me showed One Pyramid standing alone, and another scene set apart from this -- of two pyramids superimposed upon each other.

This one was the Star of David.

The two sons of Abraham were to meet after centuries of estrangement.

Time has revealed that this pre-cognition was the "miracle" meeting of Prime Minister Begin and President Sadat. It took place in the shadow of the Pyramids.

I continue to receive pre-visions of forthcoming events similar to these from time-to-time. They are uncanningly accurate.

Back to the Scene of My "Birth"

Getting back to the re-run of my immediate past life, I first saw the place and the house of my birth. In real life I had never seen or visited it. It was in Birmingham, England. I was "told" to make a "pilgrimage" there. After my recovery, this was one of the first things I did. It was there I resolved to write and publish this book.

What You "See" is What You "Get"

In "this" world, I had often complained that the life I had lived was not the life I had envisioned for myself. During and after the re-play sequences, I could see clearly that it was.

True enough, I had wanted certain things -- but I also saw I had actually "imaged" some-thing else. In asking and praying for a happy and successful life, I saw that I repeatedly "doubted" the outcome of my prayers. In other words, I "wanted" something in my "mind", but beset with doubt, I imaged something entirely different.

Doubt is "adolescent" fear. Fear is the adult version of doubt. Doubt, which leads to fear, is the "emotional" denial of our innermost desires. Fear -- aborts success and prevents us from imaging success. I saw, that just as I was about to image my most fervent desire, I would abort the image in its very borning. The image "never got off the ground." It was never completed and I never "developed" it.

I was too often "afraid" that the image I desired

could never be. I did not BELIEVE it was possible. So I
imaged the opposite -- and that which I "truly" desired
never came into "being". I discovered you get exactly
what you "see". "That which I feared -- had come upon me."

The retrospective instant re-play of my life during
that expanded time-space zero interval reified that one
dominant theme.

"THE IMAGINATION IS THE PLACE WHERE ALL THINGS HAVE THEIR
BEGINNING."

If you image it, and then develop the image, your life
will reflect the imaged picture.

In the Book of Instructions it says it this way.
"As a man thinketh in his heart (imagination) so is he."
And again, "AS YE SOW --- SO SHALL YE REAP."

———————————————

In this world, after you have sown the seed, you
have to work the "soil" to develop the harvest. It's the
same with your images. If you merely sow the seed of the
image, and do nothing to develop it, it will remain as
nothing more than a "figment of your imagination". It
will have no "roots" and will never bloom. Starting to
develop an image, and then allowing it to "wither on the
vine" as a result of doubts or fears that it really will
grow, is the reason for all our "failures".

Did you ever see a farmer harvest a "cash" crop from

a field of withered weeds?

As my past life unfolded, (and my immediate past life was the ONLY life I re-lived) I was not consciously aware of "time" limitations. The life I saw flashing past me was just as "real", just as "long" and just as "solid" as was the life I had recently left behind.

My body, (as I was subsequently to discover) was still on the hospital bed where I had left it, but at this time I was completely oblivious to its existence.

The body I was watching now was far more dynamic and alive, and I saw it growing from childhood into adulthood with every detail included -- many of which I had completely forgotten.

The entire "flashback" phase took but a "flash" from beginning to end. After I returned, I wondered whether it had all happened with the "speed of light".

Perhaps some gifted mathematician could solve the equation by dividing my "sensed" life span by the speed of light, then determine how long in terms of "Light" it did actually take for me to re-live it.

When the flashback sequences of my life were over, the next series of experiences took place. They seemed like revelations. What I "saw" and "heard" at this junction was in direct response to my searching questions. The answers I received, however, were not the answers so frequently espoused by some of the officially ordained surrogates of God. But there was a "surface" similarity.

Before I get into this phase of my out-of-body experiences however, let me share with you the details of the MIRACLE I received.

My Miracle

It was the consensus of the physicians who examined me prior to, and during my journey into the beyond, that I had suffered a "heart attack". From the trauma of it all -- they would certainly have had my endorsement of their carefully considered diagnosis. I had suffered excruciating pain, my heart stopped, and only heroic efforts to "get me back" had got it beating again. While I was away -- and again when I "came back" I PRAYED for a complete HEALING.

I prayed that my heart would be restored and returned to "perfect" and normal functioning.

AND IT WAS.

I was discharged from intensive care in three days, and out of the hospital in less than five. Subsequent examinations by the cardiologists who monitored me throughout my stay in the hospital could find <u>no traces of a heart attack or any effects from the cardiac arrest</u>. Dr. McCormick in whom I had complete confidence said it was a "unique" case. Immediately prior to discharge, my treadmill test performance was more like that of an athlete than that of a heart patient. My wife was delighted

and astonished. I was prayerfully thankful.

When I prayed, I KNEW and BELIEVED my prayers would

be answered in a positive way, because I NEVER DOUBTED

OR FEARED THAT THEY WOULD NOT BE. I have a feeling the

good doctor prayed too. I expected a "miracle" and got

one. A "miracle" is the result of doing things the way

God does them. You image exactly what you want, AND THEN

BELIEVE YOU HAVE GOT WHAT YOU IMAGED.

This is what some people call FAITH.

Jesus -- the Christ used to say -- "Oh ye of little

faith!"

This was a gentle but plain admonition to those who

"said" they wanted things so desperately -- but had little

or no "faith" they would ever get them.

Have Faith, Believe, and Do Things the
Way God Does Them

In this chapter, I would like to share this thought

with you. If you pray (ask) for what you want -- like I

prayed for what I wanted -- and you BELIEVE YOU WILL GET

WHAT YOU HAVE PRAYED FOR -- your prayers will be answered

in a positive way too.

If you pray with "half a belief" you will get what

you prayed for, and half a belief -- that just maybe

you won't -- you'll get a "double exposure" and a clouded

"negative" instead of a clear, sharp "positive".

You get what you "image". You get what you "see".
If you did the same thing with your camera -- you'd get
the same result. The waste and ruin of a good piece of film.

The formula is spelled out in no nonsense language
in the Book of Instructions. You'll find it in Mark,
Chapter 11 verse 24. This is what it says.

> "Therefore I say unto you, what things soever
> ye desire when ye pray, BELIEVE THAT YE SHALL
> RECEIVE THEM, AND YE SHALL HAVE THEM."

When I "died", I was "shown" this. I was reminded of
what He said. There is no "maybe" here. It's as "plain as
the nose on your face."

At that very instant I prayed, I BELIEVED my heart
was as good as new. I "imaged" a perfectly functioning
heart in my imagination. I saw it working -- perfect in
every detail. And it was so.

If I had doubted for one single second that such a
thing could be done -- would be done -- then it would
NOT have been so. I would have spoiled the "film".

The click of my camera would have snapped down on
an "imperfect image". My focus would be wrong, and the
developed picture would have been a fuzzy failure.

It is this doubting that "messes" everything up. It
is this same doubting that shatters all our "dreams",
(undeveloped negatives) and brings us the "opposite" of
what we really "want".

We actually image "defeat" instead of "victory".
We image "failure" instead of "success". Whatever you
image -- that's what you'll get. When the camera click
of your mind snaps, and the shutter goes down on the
"picture", that's the picture you'll develop in your life.
It can't and doesn't work any other way.

"Miracles" follow as a direct result of "imaging"
a miracle. But that's not all there is to it.

Not only must you image what you want, but you
must believe the image. Believing the image enables you
to "see" it, and as soon as you "see" it you KNOW you've
got it. That's what you say in your everyday life in
this world isn't it?

How many times have you said -- "I'll believe it when
I see it?"

I learned, and you can learn from my experience,
that your prayers will only be "answered" if you "image"
what you have prayed (asked) for. When you "see" the
image ----

BELIEVE WHAT YOU SEE

and you'll get what you see.

ALL power resides in the IMAGINATION. That's where
"God" is. That's where God image-ined you. Every "thing"
that IS, had to be "imaged" first. When the image is
developed, it comes into "being". Later, I'll share with
you how to "develop" your "image". Your imagination is
a part of God's imagination. Every-thing God image-ined
came into "being" just like you did. This is your guar-

107

antee that every thing you image-ine will come into being.

Do it the way God does it, and it'll work every time.

Image what you "want", and

> "What things soever ye desire when ye pray,
> believe that ye shall have them, and ye shall
> receive them."

This was the second powerful truth I learned BY

ACTUAL EXPERIENCE while I was "out of this world".

The first was

"THE IMAGINATION IS THE PLACE WHERE ALL THINGS HAVE THEIR

BEGINNING."

The second was

> "What things soever ye desire when ye pray,
> believe that ye shall receive them,
> and ye shall have them"

But here a word of caution is in order.

The materialization of your "image" outpictures

regardless of whether the "thing" you image is "good"

or "bad". It's also most important that you realize

that "good" and "bad" are as essential to the existence

of "this world" as is North and South, God and the

Devil, and good and evil. Remember in the Book of

Instructions Isaiah said, about "God", (chapter 45,

verse 7)

> "I form the light and create darkness:
> I create peace, and I create evil
> I the Lord do ALL these things:

Becoming

ONE thing is always in the process of becoming

another thing. The young are becoming old. The days

are becoming nights. The sinners are becoming saints.

The "bad" things in your body, so-called "germs",

"bacteria", and "viruses" are trying to "kill" you.

Your "good" antibodies are trying to stop them. The

existence of both of them make it possible for you to

stay alive -- and in fact, GUARANTEE IT.

In beautifully poetic language, the Book of Instruc-

tions tells us we have eaten of the fruit of the tree of

good and evil, and "By their fruits ye shall know them".

As human "beings" we are "both". We are "dual" in

our "nature". As long as we continue to be "human beings"

we will continue to be both "good" and "evil". But good

and evil are not what you "think" they are. As Shakespeare

said -- it's the "thinking" that makes them so. Don't

worry and fret about it. You are what you are as a

result of what you have "imaged" yourself to be.

Eve -- the other "half" of "Adam", imaged what it

would be like to "know" good and evil. Later, he too

developed his image by "eating"* the fruit of the tree

of good and evil and got exactly what he "asked" for.

In common parlance, "what you see is what you get."

Religionists and theologians tell us that God re-

wards and punishes. If you do something "good", God

will reward you. If you do something "bad", God will

punish you.

---

*The eating was the "act-ion" required to "develop"
the image.

I learned that God is not like that at all. "You" reward or punish yourself as a direct result of the IMAGES you image in your imagination. If you image something "right", you are rewarded -- you are happy. If you image something "wrong", you are punished -- you are unhappy. You make your own Heaven and your own Hell right here on earth as a result of the kind of images you develop in your imagination.

Apart from supplying the "stuff" of which Heaven and Hell is made, God has nothing to do with it. He has given you free will to create your own images. From them, you will develop your own Heaven and your own Hell.

We all like to have a "fall guy" to blame things on. We blame God for all the evils of the world -- or at least many of us do. Why doesn't God do something about war, sickness, crime, poverty and want? We never blame the person who is really responsible. I am responsible. You are responsible. Collectively, we are all responsible. We are responsible as INDIVIDUALS.

A better world and a better "me" starts with me. A better world and a better "you" starts with you. This world is a beautiful world. It's as beautiful today as the day it was created. All the blemishes that mar its pristine beauty were created by "people". People make war -- not God. Crimes are committed by people -- not God. The rivers, the streams, the lakes and the oceans are polluted by people -- not God. The earth has been despoiled by people -- not God. As "people" and as individuals, we have collectively imaged all the eyesores in this world of ours.

As individuals we constantly persist in trying to persuade other individuals to change their "wicked" ways rather than to change our own.

Saving one's own "soul" is a full time job. Trying to save other people's souls is "dreaming the impossible dream" --- however "lofty" the motivation.

I learned that the only person I can "save" is myself. Just as I can't nourish another's body by eating food for him -- I also can't image his images for him. He must do this himself.

If I want to change the world -- I must change my-self. "I" make my world what it "is". If you want to change your world -- you must change yourself. "You make your world what it "is". "I" learned there is no other way. As it says so plainly in the Book of Instructions, "I am that I am".

"I" am the way -- the truth -- and the life -- and no man cometh unto the FATHER EXCEPT BY "ME". "You" are the "I" and the "ME". No-body other than your "self" can make that statement. There is only ONE "I" and that's "YOU". You and your Father are ONE. You are the "I", and the Father of all things is in your imagination where ALL things have their beginning.

Go to the Father. Go to the imagination and image
a better you -- and a better world, -- and like a "miracle"
you will have a better you -- and a better world.

A new world and a "New you" in His image -- and yours.

The Way to "Witness"

Don't waste your time trying to save others by your
"words". Let your LIGHT shine before you -- so that others
can be guided by your light -- if that is their will.

Words grow faint and finally disappear into "space".
Your light is eternal -- and lights up space. Let your
light shine before you. It will dispel your darkness --
and show the way for others to dispel theirs.

A Few "Words about Rewards and Punishments

I learned that God doesn't reward or punish you.
He doesn't reward you with a passport to Heaven or
punish you with a passport to Hell. You reward or
punish yourself. You make your own Heaven and your
own Hell. You do these things as a result of the images
you imagine.

But be careful about the "rewards" you image for
yourself. They often turn out to be "punishments".
"Body sensed" rewards lead to body sensed punishments.

You _can_ reward your earthly "accomplishments" by rewarding yourself with a stiff drink. If you reward your "self" too often for too many accomplishments, you can punish yourself with a stiff case of alcoholism.

If the reward of big meal for things "well done" becomes a "habit", you can become a habitual glutton.

Don't get your rewards and punishments out of focus. The picture can easily become a distortion of your original image. "Self" reward is a difficult thing to control.

"Pray to your Father which is in secret -- and your Father will REWARD you openly". (The Book of Instructions) Change "gears". Quit trying to "reward" yourself -- it often turns out to be a "bummer". Leave it to God to reward you. Don't be as the hypocrites are. Don't self reward yourself with the self endowed -- self proclained title of "born again".

Your Light which shines from within you will speak far more loudly than your "words".

The world will "see" that you are born again. There will be no need to proclaim it with "words".

Chapter Nine

WHAT IS SIN?

Sin is making the wrong decision -- imaging the
wrong image. God's Universe -- and yours, operates accord-
ing to specific, inviolable, "laws". These laws never
change. Like God -- they are the only things that never
change. They always work the same way.

When you image any picture in your imagination--you
do so within the framework of these laws. If you image
some-thing which is not "lawful", it is a sin. The image
is wrong and the picture is wrong. However, just like
all images, it will materialize -- and you will suffer the
penalty of the law you have violated. You will be "punished".
God does not punish you -- you punish yourself as a
direct result of the unlawful images you imagine. The
Book of Instructions tells you what these laws are.
Later on I will share the meaning of these laws with you
just as they were shared with me.

As long as you persist in imaging pictures that are
unlawful, you will be punishing yourself. When you "realize" -- by the results you receive -- long--or short term,
that you have committed a sin, you must "repent". Repent
means to change, so you change your unlawful images into
"lawful" images.

Immediately, you do this, and you are "forgiven" and

rewarded. There is no need to wear sackcloth and ashes. No need to put yourself on display before the "world" and give a "testimony" of your "sins".

Pray to the Father in secret -- and He will "reward" you openly.

Do It the Way God Does It

When you were born, in addition to the other "gifts" God gave you -- He gave you an imagination. Your imagination has no "limits" because your imagination is a part of God's imagination -- in the same way a drop of water from the ocean is a part of the entire ocean.

The qualities and potentialities of your imagination are exactly the same as the qualities and potentialities of God's imagination. God will share His imagination with you to the extent you believe He will.

If you believe this, then

> "What things soever ye desire when ye pray, believe that ye receive them, and ye shall have them".

Desiring and praying is the same thing. The two "words" are used interchangably in the paragraph above. You can desire and pray for anything you can "imagine". Then if you BELIEVE you will get it by "seeing" it in clear, sharp, focus on the television screen of your mind, "ye shall have it".

All you need to do now is to "develop" the picture

until it materializes. Man's "one-step" cameras do this
every day. You can do it every day too. The process
involved is exactly the same process that brought you
into being. God made you in His image. He saw that
the image was good. He focused and "formed" you -- and
you were made into a perfect likeness of His image. By
using the same imagination God used to create you, you
can become a co-creator with God by imaging your images
and bringing them into being.

But you must BELIEVE THIS.

God said

> "What things soever ye desire when ye pray,
> BELIEVE ye shall receive them and ye shall
> have them."

I didn't say it -- God did, and everything God said came
to pass.

At this point, let me summarize two of the three
truths that were shared with me while I was out of this
world.

First,

"THE IMAGINATION IS THE PLACE WHERE ALL THINGS HAVE THEIR

BEGINNING"

Second,

> "What things soever ye desire when ye pray,
> believe that ye shall receive them and ye
> shall have them."

There was a third truth however, which, when exercised
in conjunction with the other two, guarantees production

and delivery of your developed images.

I will share this with you in the next chapter.

Chapter Ten

THE MAGIC POWER OF BELIEVING

Believing takes something we call Faith. Jesus
Christ often began his discourses with the words "Oh
ye of little faith". Faith has been described as "the
substance of things hoped for -- but not yet seen".

But Faith isn't enough. You need Faith -- and more.
You need to "ACT". Act is a word which denotes "MOTION"
and motion is LIGHT. You have to bring light to bear on
the image you have imagined. In "this world", when you
snap your camera shutter on the image you have selected,
you need one other ingredient to obtain a clear, sharp
picture, you need LIGHT.

Focusing your camera on the image you have selected -
and then not activating the shutter will get you "nothing". You must ACT and work to develop your image. The
operative Law here is "Faith without works is Dead". It's
right there in the Book of Instructions. After God had
imaged the "world", He ACTED. He WORKED "for six days,"
and rested on the "seventh". On the seventh day He saw
the wonderful results of His "works" and pronounced it
"good". Apart from the beautiful poetic language used,
the words plainly indicate that God WORKED.

To get the kind of self -- and the kind of world you

want, you must WORK too.

You must do three things. First you must image what you want. Second you must BELIEVE you will get what you have imaged. Third you must ACT your part and WORK to develop your image. Only then will you "receive it". You must do all the things you have the "power" to do. God will do all those things only He has the power to do. Like the restoration of my "Heart". We call the things we can't do -- and which God does for us -- MIRACLES.

When asked about the miracles He did, Jesus the Christ said -- "It is not I that doeth these things -- it's the Father within me."

There are many things you were created to do -- that you SHOULD do. Miracles are not among them. The miracles will be done by the Father that is within you.

If you fail to do the things you were created to do. If you fail to "work" on the image you have imaged. If you fail to develop the "negative" into a "positive", your "picture" will never "materialize".

The faith you exercise in your "believing", and the "works" that you do are the "labor pains" which develop into the "substance" and the "birth" of your new creation. You were created in the image of God. You are a part of, and an extension of God in the same way the plough -- a creation of man, is an extension of man.

When you carry out the WORK God created you to do, the image you have imaged will be "born" and brought into "being". If you fail to do your WORK and your "part" in

the scheme of things -- your image will die "aborning".

It will never "see" the Light of day. Your image will

never become more than a mere figment of your imagination.

I was admonished not to dream "impossible dreams".

I was told to play the part in THIS life that was

written into the script for me to play.

The playright -- whom we call "God", is in total charge

of the entire production. In my role as a co-creator

(or co-producer) I learned I should play my part to the

very best of my ability. When I reached the point where

I was playing my part to perfection -- I would be given

a "bigger" part to play. I was impressed with the

realization that my present role gave me an opportunity

to express all the abilities (talents)   I was capable of

expressing at this juncture of my earthly existence.

(I believe your role provides you with the same fulness

of expression). The scope of any future role would be

restricted only by my ability to perceive the totality

of the grand design. It was not my function to image the

"scenery". The mountains, the oceans, and the flora and

fauna of the Universe was the backdrop God had so

wonderfully and generously provided. This was the stage

upon which the entire drama would be enacted. My role

was an integral and vital part of the whole play. I

was told that I should image every image I could imagine

that would enhance and compliment the scene and the setting
in which I found myself.

I should develop my "part" to its full potential --
and to take "no thought for the morrow". God would provide all I needed to make my part a success. But -- I
must "work" at it.

Faith that I could play the part, and Faith that
God would play His part was not enough. I must work on
my part until I had perfected it. "Faith without works
is dead".

Image your image. Believe you will receive it, and
work as though you have already got it. This "work" is
the supreme test of your Faith.

Then -- as a part of, and an extension of God, you
can say with the Christ -- "it is not I that doest these
things, it's the Father within me". The Father and I
are ONE.

The Truth Has Never Changed

There is, of course, nothing "new" about any of these
things I have shared with you. It's been this way since
the beginning of "time". It's all been said before --
but since hardly anybody ever listens -- somebody has to
keep repeating it. Each one that repeats it says it a little
differently. They use different "words".

Christ stated all these truths almost 2,000 years ago.

He stated them BEFORE He died -- and proved them when He
"came back". Thomas -- the DOUBTER didn't BELIEVE Him.

Many still don't believe. But believe me -- if you
put into practice what I have shared with you since I
came back -- you will discover as I did that

"THE IMAGINATION IS THE PLACE WHERE ALL THINGS HAVE THEIR

BEGINNING."

That,

> "What things soever ye desire when ye pray,
> believe ye shall receive them and ye shall
> have them."

And that,

all you need to do is to supply the Faith and
the Works -- because without them,

"Faith without Works is Dead."

In actual practice -- if you image a new home, -- see
the picture on the television screen of your mind. See it
in detail. Then start immediately to "construct it." See
it complete on the wooded lot. Work out the color scheme.
Buy a door knocker for the front door. See yourself
and your family living in it. Then have the faith and
go to work.

As you draw nearer to God -- God will draw nearer to
you. As you draw nearer to your developed image -- your
developed image will draw nearer to you.

Think on these things -- and BELIEVE.

The real SIN is not BELIEVING.

Chapter Eleven

HOW MY DEATH CHANGED MY LIFE

This is NOT a religious book. The religious references in it are pertinent to -- and a part of -- the total experiences I lived through while I was "dead".

To most of us, the matter of life and death is a "religious" matter. My religious upbringing was what many would describe as an "orthodox" one. I always had questions about whether it was the "right" one, and my journey to the "other" world vindicated the validity of my questions. It was not until I died that my questions were answered -- then I learned how it really was.

The people on whom I had relied for the truth -- hadn't "been there" to discover the truth. They taught me what they THOUGHT the Book of Instructions said.

I discovered there was indeed a thin veneer of truth in what they promulgated -- but it wasn't the Truth, the whole Truth and nothing but the Truth. Perhaps you heard the Methodist interpretation -- or the Catholic -- or the Episcopalian.

To really know -- it's necessary to have "been there". If you don't know where the treasure is -- you can't guide others to it. My experiences made it easy for me to

recognize the obvious sincerity of what they said --
but for the most part, their interpretations are
only skin deep. Others are just simply a "cop out".
People everywhere are still hungry for the truth.
"Sinners" filled with feelings of heavy guilt grasp at
the **straws** they hold out, and after a quick emotional "fix"
find themselves as hungry as before. Their descriptions
of God as a man -- whose "arms" were reaching "down" to
hold me up is poetic, romantic and wrong. God is not a
man -- but everything they tell you infers and implies
that He is.

I use the word "He" and "Him" as a reading con-
venience. God has no "sex" as we understand and use the
term. The imaged motion dividing the ONE is sex!

God is not a man. God is in, and IS your imagination.
He "resides" there as the ONE POWER that makes all things
happen. This has nothing to do with "religion". This is
the way things are.

I was told -- and perhaps you were too, that Jesus--
the Christ came into the world as the Son of God. He
often referred to Himself as the Son of Man. I learned
He was both. He was the Son of God -- and the Son of Man.

The Book of Instructions indicated He had brothers
and sisters. They too were the sons and daughters of
God and of man. You and I are the sons and daughters
of God and of man. God made us out of Himself. Without
Him -- "nothing was made".

These new truths came to me while I was dead -- and
they changed my life. I saw the truth as it really is --
and not as the professional providers of the truth tell
us it is. I learned that God imaged and imagined you
and I. He is the Father -- we are His children.

The Christ of His-tory did live. He was the son of
God. He did die for our "sins". He still "dies" for our
sins. He was crucified. He was buried -- and He did
"rise" from the dead. But that's not all. Christ was and
is a part of the same God that you and I are a part of.
God made Christ -- and you and me out of Himself. We
crucify the Christ within us every time we deny the
"Light" and embrace the "dark". We crucify Him every
time we "sin", every time we image the "wrong" image,
We raise Him from the dead every time we "repent" (change)
and image the "right" instead of the "wrong".

The part of God that we are, IS the Christ. The
living Christ was and is "the light of the world." Christ
is the light that God created in each one of us. Christ
is the Light that "lighteth every man that cometh into
the world". The Christ part in us is the Divine part in
us. Christ lives in each one of us today as the light
of our life just as the Christ of His-tory lived almost
2,000 years ago. The light was exemplified as the light
of the world in the body of a man who was the son of man
and the Son of God.

His "birth" also exemplifies what His Father told

us in the Book of Instructions. God gave us a living

proof of His statement of Truth when He said

>"Therefore I say unto you
>What soever things ye desire when ye pray,
>believe ye shall receive them and ye shall
>have them."

That same "Christ", that same man, the light that

lighteth every man that cometh into the world "dev-

eloped" and perfected Himself until he became ALL LIGHT.

He was the son of man when He cried "My God, My God,

why has thou forsaken Me?" He was the Son of God when

He said to Satan "Get thee behind Me". To fulfill the

command "Be ye perfect even as your Father which is in

Heaven is perfect," He imaged perfection and became what

He imaged. His-story in the Book of Instructions is the

story of His Faith and His works.

Christ is the Light of the World and God's Only Begotten Son

In the beginning -- all was dark and void. And God

said "let there be light" -- and there was light. Accord-

ing to the Book of Instructions, "Christ is the light that

cometh out of the Darkness". This light -- this Christ,

was God's first and only "begotten son". When the Christ

of HIS-tory "appeared", He came to exemplify the light

that lighteth every man that cometh into the world.

When you and I were born, the Christ, the light

that cometh out of the Darkness, "entered" into us and became the Light of our life. He -- the light, IS our life. There is no need to "ask Christ to come into your life -- He is already there. All you need to do is to "recognize" He is there, and let His light burn on the "altar" within you.

"Know ye not that ye are the temple of the Living God?"

Learning these things was how my death changed my life. I learned that this Christ -- this light of the world -- does indeed light every man that cometh into the world. And every woman too!

When I died, this light -- this same light, was the light that left my body. "I" had left my body. "I" had gone to be with my Father. Then all became "dark and void" as far as my body was concerned. In death, I discovered that "I" was the light that lit up my darkness. It was the wee, small light in the long dark tunnel, which became the big, all engulfing Light at the end of the "tunnel". Let me share something else I learned.

When you are "born" and you take your first* breath -- the light that cometh out of the darkness comes in. When you "die" and take your last breath -- "you", the light, go out. You leave your body. It is just as simple as that. There is no need for a lot of "mumbo jumbo". There is no need for pomp and circumstance. None of this had

---

* "And God breathed the breath of life into man and man became a living soul."

ever provided me with the truth. I had to go <u>where</u> the
truth was in order to KNOW <u>what</u> the truth was. That is
not to say you should not go to church. But you must
know that singing beautiful hymns and being a member of
the choir won't buy you a ticket to heaven. You could
do a lot worse than going to church -- but you could
also do a lot better. In addition to going to church,
you can go where God is ---- INSIDE YOUR OWN BEING. There
you will meet Christ -- "the Light of your life" face to
face.

He is there right now -- and has always been there.
"Be still and know that "I" am God".

"The Kingdom of Heaven is within you".

How you are forgiven and Why you must pay your "debts"

Allowing someone else to pay my "debts" or suffer for
the "sins" I had committed was a concept that had always
deeply offended the conscience God had given me.

I learned He'd made a law to cover these things --
a law that will never be changed or abrogated by Him or
anyone else. If indeed it was changed or abrogated --
it would never have been a law to begin with.
That law is

"As ye sow -- so shall ye reap."

It is and was the law on which the very Universe is
founded. Mercy and grace were built into this law by

its total justice and total simple honesty.

If you image and then commit a "sin", the materialization of that image would -- in and of itself "show"
you the error of your ways by its results. "By their fruits
shall ye KNOW them". "Mercy and justice and grace" are
yours for the "asking" by the repenting (changing) of
your sinful image into a "right"-eous image. What more
gracious kind of forgiveness could God give you. You
cancel out your "wrong" by substituting a "right". What
could possibly be more fair -- or more just?
It exemplifies the law

"As ye sow -- so shall ye reap"
In death, I was shown that we are -- each one of us, totally
responsible for our own "sins". We can't in good conscience
lay them on another. We can't in the name of justice,
expect anyone else to suffer in our stead. All the
legal statutes of our civilization are based on God's
law, but God's law is more merciful. He never brands us
as unredeemable criminals -- and never throws away the
key. We imprison ourselves by the kind of images we image
and what we "do". We free ourselves by "repenting"
(changing) our image(s) in order to "undo" what we have
done. Any fair and rational minded person would, I am
sure, agree with this. I learned that God would have it
no other way. It was impressed upon me that there are no
loopholes in God's law.

A law with a loophole is no law at all.

The incessantly repeated misinterpretation that you and I can commit all the crimes in the decalogue -- and then escape "scot free" by just merely believing that Christ died on the cross to "save" us from paying for our sins provides the most horrendous loophole of all.

It is the ultimate in unlawful imaging. When we allow ourselves to image such a picture -- the picture is incomplete. It's only "half" of the truth. While it is true that we are "forgiven" in "God's" world, we still owe a debt in man's world. The debt to "this world" must be repaid to balance the forgiveness we receive in the "other world".

In the Book of Instructions, we are informed we shall "pay to the uttermost farthing". "As we sow -- so shall we reap". The man-made abberation that we can "beat the rap" by placing the burden of our crimes on a fall guy "up there" and "get away with it," nullifies every law God made. It's the biggest "cop out" of all time. The belief that vicarious atonement will get you "off the hook" is nothing more than a free pass to a fools paradise.

The only time we truly feel at peace is when we have "balanced the books", when we have paid back what we owe.

Christ did "die" for our "sins" 2,000 years ago. He still "dies" for them today. But it's the Christ within us that dies today just as He did "yesterday".

He died within Peter, one of Christ's closest friends, who in spite of constant advice from Him, deliberately made wrong decisions. He conjured up images he thought would provide an alibi for his "sins". He lied shamelessly -- and repeated one of his lies three times. When he was asked whether he "knew" Christ, he "denied" Him. We too "deny" Christ every time we refuse to "identify" Him within us. Christ is the light within us, "The light that lighteth every man that cometh into the world". We "pay" for these "sins" like Peter paid for his sins. He too was "crucified" on the cross -- UPSIDE DOWN.

Like Peter, we too persist in "seeing" everything UPSIDE DOWN. And as long as we persist -- we -- like Christ will be nailed to the cross we voluntarily choose to carry on our back. Judas, another close confidant -- who collected and kept the money - also betrayed Him. He took a bribe for fingering his friend. He was struck by remorse -- and subsequently paid for his sins just like Peter. He hanged himself. Not exactly the nicest way to go. He suffered in his own self-made Hell before he paid the ultimate price.

Joan of Arc, after confessing her "sins" to God, to Christ, and to a Christian Ecclesiastical Court, was burned at the stake by men who preached and promulgated this same pernicious doctrine. His-tory is replete with other deaths of the body even more hideous than crucifixion, but God neither planned or premeditated any of them.

The death of the body and of the "soul" is planned and premeditated as a result of the images men image in their imagination. Joan of Arc was found innocent of defeating the British -- but guilty of wearing men's clothes! She was burned to death at the stake as a result of the images "Christian" men held at that time.

If those images had not been "changed", almost every "modern" civilized woman in the world would be just as guilty today. Wearing a pants-suit doesn't make you a "fallen" woman.

When the image is changed -- the world we "live" in is changed. If you and I want the kind of world God imaged for us, (and pronounced it good) but which we have degraded by our own images, we must change our individual images.

There is no way one individual can image for another. There is no way we can avoid suffering for our own unlawful images. "As we sow -- so shall we reap". Just as long as we judgementally try to persuade others to change their ways -- without changing ours, so long will this sorry world of ours continue to "exist". Vicarious atonement is unlawful and a mere "figment of the imagination".

The law is "As ye sow -- so shall ye reap".

The Still Living Christ

We crucify the Christ within us everytime we "sin" and saddle Him with our sins. He lives again every time we repent and change the image from wrong to right. Of course, when we image something wrong -- we don't really know what we are doing -- until it hits us where it hurts. On the cross, Christ said "Forgive them for they know not what they do".* The last thing He said was -- "IT IS FINISHED". He had finished something we must all "finish". He had followed the script God wrote, and played His part to perfection. God said

> "Be ye therefore perfect -- even as your
> Father which is in heaven is perfect."

This brings me full circle to the words that small child said to me.

*"Do you grown-ups really know what you are
 doing?"

Chapter Twelve

REFLECTIONS

The following is a resume of the most salutory
features of my out of the body experiences. First,
"THE IMAGINATION IS THE PLACE WHERE ALL THINGS HAVE THEIR
BEGINNING."

It's the "womb" where ALL creations are created. It's the
matrix of the Cosmos. It's the Kingdom of Heaven. It's
where "God" is. It's where God lives, moves and has His
"being". God will, and does share His imagination with
us to the extent we ask Him to share it. His invitation
is forthright and unmistakable.

"Ask and ye shall receive, knock and it shall be
opened unto you". You can and will receive every "thing"
you ask for and image. This is His guarantee.

> "What things soever ye desire when ye pray,
> BELIEVE ye shall receive them, and ye shall
> have them."

This includes every "thing". That which is "lawful" and
that which is "unlawful". In "orthodox" terminology, the
"good" things come from "God" and the "bad" things come
from the "Devil". In reality, they both come from God.
God said in Isaiah chapter 45 verse 7:

> "I form the light, and create darkness;
> I create peace and I create evil:
> I the Lord do all these things."

The first step in "praying" or asking for what

you want is to know exactly what it is you do want.
A "fuzzy" image is not good enough. You must focus
in on a clear, sharp, well-defined "object" -- just
as you would with a camera. That's the only way you'll
obtain a perfect "picture". The picture you see on the
television screen of your mind is the "negative". Now-
it needs developing. You do this by "believing" you
already have what you have imaged. This is the "jel-
ling" process. You do this with the same assurance as
you do when you take a picture with a "One-Step" Camera.
When you snap the shutter -- you "know" you have got it.
Act with the same assurance when you image an object in
your imagination. You will learn -- just as I did -- by
BELIEVING and DOING it. If what you get -- is not exactly
what you want -- it's because your image was "blurred".
You'll get the same fidelity "out" as you put "in."

A blurred image will get you a blurred picture. You'll
get exactly what you "see". You develop your image by the
ACT of believing. Believing is the "jell" that transforms
and develops a "negative" into a "positive". Without
BELIEF, your image remains just a "figment" of your imagination. It never materializes. It never "develops".
Development of your image is the third and final step in
the realization of your image.

Then, in full Faith that "GOD" will deliver what He
has promised, thank Him in ADVANCE.

The way to do this is to

> "Enter into thy closet, and when thou hast
> shut thy door, thank God in secret -- and
> He will REWARD thee OPENLY".

Here are a few helpful words of advice that were given

to me. "Don't keep on keeping on". Don't keep

praying the same prayer over and over again.

God isn't deaf -- and He has 20-20- vision. If

your prayer isn't answered, YOU are doing something

wrong. Start all over again. Form a perfect image

of what you want, then believe you have already received

it. You have planted the "seed". <u>Don't keep digging it

up to see if it's growing</u>. That's DOUBT -- <u>and with

doubt in the picture</u>, it will never grow. It will take

root, grow and flower only when you "fertilize" it with

the magic of believing.

Don't fret and worry.

> "Your Father knoweth what things you have
> need of before ye ask".

He is there "within" waiting for you to "ask". "Asking"

is the part you must play. Play your part -- get your

lines right -- and don't "worry".

Worry begets doubt, and doubt destroys belief.

"As ye sow -- so shall you reap".

Plant your seed image. Water it with Faith and

Harvest it with Belief.

To succeed, the following is your absolute and unchangeable guarantee -----

> "Whatsoever things ye desire when ye pray,
> <u>believe ye shall receive them</u> and ye shall
> have them."

Special Note

Those readers who have questions

---or who would like to schedule a speaking date

for the author
should contact

AMERICAN BIO CENTER
P.O.Box 473
Williamsburg, Va 23187
Tel 804-725-2234
Fax 804-725-2234

ADDENDUM

QUESTIONS and ANSWERS

DURING THE PROCESS OF PROOFREADING, THE PEOPLE INVOLVED
WERE SO INTERESTED IN THE TEXT THEY BEGAN TO ASK QUESTIONS.
YOU MAY HAVE SOME TOO. HERE ARE THE QUESTIONS
THEY ASKED——AND HERE ARE MY ANSWERS.

YOUR QUESTIONS MAY BE DIFFERENT——AND IF YOU INQUIRE——I
WILL ANSWER YOURS AS WELL. NATURALLY, SINCE I WILL BE USING
"WORDS" YOUR INTERPRETATION OF THOSE WORDS MAY STILL NOT
ANSWER YOUR QUESTIONS TO YOUR ENTIRE SATISFACTION——BUT DON'T
LET THAT PREVENT YOU FROM ASKING.

YOUR QUESTIONS ARE WELCOMED.

Q. How does one believe?

A. It's strange, but true, that most people need "proof" before
they "believe." Paraphrasing Jesus, He said "don't look for signs
and wonders." Or putting it another way, don't look for "proofs."
Proof without belief is an impossibility, even in the physical
world. Alexander Graham Bell had no "proof" his telephone would
"work," he just "believed" it would work. All great discoveries
and "inventions" were presaged by "belief." The working "proof"
followed the "belief," not the other way around.

One word of warning however. If your belief is based on err-
oneous concepts it will NOT become a working, physical proof.
If the image is wrong, the results will be wrong. If the results
are not what you wanted them to be, go back to the drawing
board and design a new image. Don't waste time "blaming"
something or somebody. If you hit your thumb with a hammer
while driving a nail, don't blame the hammer. Your vision,
or image of where the nail was -----was wrong.

Form a perfect image, believe the image, and the "proof" will
appear before your eyes.

Believing, like imaging, takes practice, and practice makes
perfect.

Q. What do you, Harry Hone, mean by "death".

A. By death, I mean death of the body. YOU do not die. It's your body that dies. But even your body doesn't die in the usually accepted sense of the word. It merely CHANGES. It becomes something else. YOU remain what YOU have always been. YOU remain LIGHT. Total light. YOU escape from the confining "imprisonment" of the body. YOU are freed from the "life sentence" TO WHICH YOU WERE COMMITTED AT BIRTH. Every hour of every day was an opportunity to get time off for "good behaviour". Every minute of every hour was an opportunity to "learn your lines" and perfect your part. "Life" as we know it, is like serving an apprenticeship. We just can't become a Master, until we have served and completed our apprenticeship. In this modern day world of ours, nobody seems to want to "serve" an apprenticeship. Everyone seems to want to become a Master right away. "Life" is a learning process. Death is a "resting" process. When we have rested, we will be called upon to start learning again. To do this, you will need a body again. God will provide you with as many as you need until you finish the job. When the apprentice pleases the Master, you will be able to say with Jesus, "IT IS FINISHED".

Q. Is there any reason why you did not publish your book right away?

A. Yes there is. During that period of time I spent in the other world, the world of Light, I was programmed with an avalanche of new knowledge, and given a number of "missions" to complete.

THE MOST PLEASURABLE OF THESE "MISSIONS", ONE THAT APPEARED TO BE ALMOST IMPOSSIBLE OF CONSUMMATION WAS THE DISCOVERY OF MY SISTER AT THE ANTIPODES OF THIS EARTH OF OURS.

DURING THE SEPARATION OF ME FROM MY BODY, I WAS TOLD IN A SILENT AND WORDLESS "VOICE" EXACTLY WHERE TO FIND HER. I BELIEVED I WOULD FIND HER—I NEEDED NO PROOF—AND I DISCOVERED HER TO BE EXACTLY WHERE I WAS TOLD SHE WOULD BE—AND THIS CAME TRUE AFTER AN ABSENCE OF NOT KNOWING WHERE SHE WAS FOR MORE THAN THIRTY FOUR YEARS. THE FOLLOWING DETAILS AND DOCUMENTATION THAT FOLLOW SHOULD EXPLAIN EVERYTHING. THE OUTWORKING AND MATERIALIZATION OF THIS AMAZING "MESSAGE" WAS GIVEN ME AFTER I HAD "ASKED FOR IT", BELIEVED I WOULD RECEIVE IT, AND AFTER I HAD DISCOVERED

THE LIGHT AT THE END OF THE TUNNEL.

SOME FAMILY BACKGROUND

I am the eldest of four children born to Harry and Ada Hone. We were all born in England. There were three brothers and one sister. My sister's name is Dulcie, a musically Anglicized variation of Dolce. As I remembered her she was as sweet as her name. We all grew up and married in England. Then came World War II. We were all scattered to the four points of the compass while it lasted, and in it's aftermath, our separation was aggravated even more. Dulcie and her husband and children emigrated to Australia. The last written communication I received from her was dated June 1949. I attempted to contact her without success during the ensuing thirty plus years of our separation. After almost a half life-time of total silence I began to despair of ever hearing from her again. There was no way of knowing whether she was "alive" or "dead." But deep down "inside," my desire to "find" her never "died." Like all true desires, I took this one with me when I left this world. While I was "gone" I "asked" how I could find her. Along with my other questions I was "programmed" with the answer. I did exactly what I was programmed to do at the time

I was programmed to do it. I wrote to the Courier Mail in Brisbane, Australia. I informed them of my mission and they generously printed my appeal. I also enclosed a photograph of Dulcie and myself taken more than thirty five years ago while I was serving in the Royal Air Force.

Everything was right on target. The response was instantaneous. A cable from Dulcie completed the Australian connection. The cable was followed by a telephone call which effectively ended a vacuum of silence and separation.

My prayers had been answered, Dulcie was "found".

The "belief" had produced the "proof".

Once again,

> "Whatsoever things ye desire when ye pray,
>
> <u>believe</u> ye shall receive them, and ye shall
>
> have them".

A Letter <u>From</u> the Editor.

Queensland Newspapers Pty. Ltd.

BRISBANE

THE COURIER-MAIL
TELEGRAPH
THE SUNDAY MAIL

TELEGRAMS AND CABLES
"COURIER-MAIL" BRISBANE
G.P.O. BOX 130, 4001
TELEPHONE: 52 6011

Dear Mr. Hone,

Thank you for your
recent letter.

Your photograph, and
the article which ran in The
Courier-Mail on December 4 are
returned (as requested).

We hope this helps
you in the search for your
sister.

Sincerely,

(Mrs) M Pascoe

Editor's A/Secretary

Encl (2):

<u>Author's Note</u>. It did indeed help! The search was a complete
success.

The "discovery" of where God was -- led to the discovery of

where "Dulcie" was. "Seek and ye shall find" -- "Knock and

it shall be opened unto you."

It's all there in the book of instructions!

Q. What do you mean by the word Light?

A. Light is the first expression of God. You cannot "see"
Light. Light is THAT which enables you to "see".
You cannot see God. Light is motion, the fastest motion of
which we are "aware". As light "slows" down it "becomes" something
else. Everything is "descended" from Light. God described
Christ as "the Light that Lighteth every man that cometh into
the world".

Light is that which is the Life within us. Light, Life and LOVE
are synonymous in word terms. They are a Divine Trinity. They
are three aspects of the ONE.

Light is that which is breathed into you when you are "born",
when you see the light of day.

"And God breathed the breath of Life into man, and man became
a living soul".

Love is the DESIRE part of the Trinity. The light within your
body is the life within your body, and when your Light goes out,
your life goes out. Then as far as "this world" is concerned
you "see" no thing. I found this to be the truth, the whole truth,
and nothing but the truth when my light went out.

In my case, my "part" in the drama of life wasn't completed.
I made an exit to the "wings" while I still had some lines to
say. However, as you can see, I was brought back to finish my
role and complete my part of the script.

Some of those lines and part of that script are in this book.
After reading the lines and studying the script, I hope you too
will find the light which is the real YOU. You can then say with
Jesus "The father and I are One".

Q. Do you believe there was a real, live, physical Jesus Christ?

A. Yes I do. History teaches us that Jesus Christ was named Joseph-Bar-Joseph by the Hebrews of His day, the Christos by the Greeks, and Jesus by the Romans. During my journey to where Jesus is now, I learned He is still the Light of the World. His earthly father's name was Joseph, His heavenly Father was God, and his earthly mother was Mary. Jesus, the eternal Light of the World is within each one of us. When we roll the stone away from our bodily sepulcher, the Light will replace the darkness. As long as the stone is there we will never see the Light. Our task is to remove it. When we do, we will see the Christ. He is the Light of the World.

Q. Was Jesus the Son of God?

A. Yes He was, but he constantly referred to Himself as the Son of Man. The God part of Christ was the Light within. The God part of us is the Light within.

When Christ was born from His earthly mother He was full of Light. The "wise" men saw that light and "followed" it. But following the Light is not enough. You have to LIVE the Light, by living the Life, and living the Life as Jesus lived His Life is the only Way, the only Truth, and the only Life. If your life is anything less than His----you must be born again. Being born again is not the end---it's merely another beginning.

Q. I noticed while reading your manuscript that you say that the Light will leave the body when the body is no longer a fit habitation. You go on to say that this same Light will at some future time enter into a new body? Is this what most people call reincarnation?

A. As I have tried to make clear many times, the WORDS are not the things they try to describe or explain. Reincarnation is a word, and it is generally used as a "trigger" word. Its use automatically "triggers" resistance. I avoid this word and use, when I must, the word re-birth.

Re-birth means nothing more or less than being born again. The entire Christian faith is established and grounded on an unswerving belief in "re-birth." The believers are convinced beyond any possible doubt that the Saviour will appear again as a result of yet another "birth." When we come into "this" world from the "other" world we are said to be "born." I was programmed with the belief that Jesus will indeed be born again---in the flesh as well as in the "spirit." Of course in "reality" there are not two separate worlds. There is only ONE WORLD. One is visible to the senses--the other is invisible to the senses. Jesus Christ is in the world now. He is in that "part" of the world where body sensed seekers are unable to find him. To those who seek Him in the "spirit"--He is always present. Jesus said to Nicodemus "Ye must be born again." I discovered that we must be born again --------- until we learn by constant repetition that the admonition "Be ye therefore perfect" is not an exercise in futility.

Man will appear in a different "body" just as Christ will

appear in a different "body."

Reincarnation and "body" are just words. They mean different

things to different people. Don't get hung up on words. Words

are not what they try to describe or explain. Try selling the

idea of Soviet "democracy" to a believer in American "democracy."

You'll have quite a job on your hands. It may even lead to

an atomic war----and you couldn't get any further apart than

that!

Q. Your manuscript doesn't say so in as many words, but is

the Light the same thing as the soul?

A. We're back again to "words." Words are the embodiment of

the Tower of Babel. I choose not to use the word "soul"

because it is so widely misunderstood. People want to know

how big it is. How much it weighs. What part of the body

conceals its location--and so on. Light is far more accept-

able. People can visualize Light more easily than they can

soul. I have no quarrel with anyone who wants to quiet their

mind by interchanging these two words. Whichever word is

chosen, the Truth will remain the same.

Render unto Caesar the things that are Caesar's, and unto

God the things that are God's.

Q. Thank you for inviting me to read your manuscript. I read

it twice. At the first reading I concluded you were against

the "orthodox" view of the Christian religion. "Are you?"

A. Of course not. So-called "orthodoxy" in the Christian

religion is in a constant state of flux. What was orthodox

yesterday is unorthodox today.

If we believe that a thousand years is but a "day", then

orthodoxy is but a passing "phase". So-called orthodox

religion is a passing phase through which we all travel

on our way to the Truth. When we are "bound" to orthodoxy

we are not free. Only the Truth will make us free.

The orthodox Christian religion is man's organized 'sense'

of God. Its various interpretations are as diverse and

devisive as its denominations.

Beyond and above this battleground of beliefs and the

warfare of words is the Truth. Once we have reached this

rarified atmosphere we can look with compassion and under-

standing upon the struggle we all have to overcome.

Christ's disciples were at odds about His "teachings" as

are His disciples of today. My journey into the beyond

made these things very clear to me. I am simply sharing

with you those things I learned, without in any way asking

you to subscribe to them or their "authenticity".

Listen to the STILL, small voice within for the Truth

that will make you free. I am no prophet, neither do I

claim to possess the key that unlocks the door behind which

lies the truth. I merely had a unique experience during

which these "impressions" became a part of my consciousness.

If some would say after reading my manuscript that it all

comes from my imagination--I would be the first to agree.

The most indelible impression etched upon my consciousness

during my two minute odyssey in the other world was-----

THE IMAGINATION IS THE PLACE WHERE ALL THINGS HAVE THEIR

BEGINNING!

Q. What IS the Imagination?

A. It's the 0*(the zero) from which issues the 1.

Q. Is there such a thing as God's grace?

A. Yes. But the "word" grace is not the "thing" it seeks

to describe or explain. Grace comes from God when it is

needed and is "asked" for. Remember also that God is a

word, and is not that which the word seeks to describe or

explain.

Read Genesis Chapter 1. It is a "record" of what GOD "<u>said</u>".

It begins, "And God <u>said</u> "let there be light--and there

was light." But the "word" God spoke, was not the light

God created. God's "word" was the "image" He "imagined."

The imagination from which <u>all</u> images emerge is the 'womb'

of <u>all</u> creation.

The "word" is the <u>invisible</u> image, the result is the

<u>visible</u> creation.

The "word" grace, is the invisible image you imagine, the

resultant grace is the visible grace God <u>delivers</u>.

* Zero. Another "word" which deserves better treatment than I have given to it above. Your dictionary will tell you that "zero" means "nothing"——"nil". Yet without it our numerical system would be meaningless and inoperative. In truth,it signifies the <u>invisible</u> "void" from which emerges the <u>visible</u> materialization of our system of numbers.

The word "zero" in fact is a mathematical representation of the beginning of all "things". Zero is a "void" in the same way that " In the beginning——the earth was without form and void". From this "void" without "form" God created <u>everything</u>. In the same way that the "void" of zero "O" was the womb out of which all other numbers emerged, so was the "void" described in the Book of Instructions the womb out of which the entire Universe was created.

Everything that there IS——is created from an apparent "nothing"——the——"O"——. and from that ——"O"——comes the first visible something——LIGHT.

It is from this LIGHT that we are "descended". We are the "LIGHT that LIGHTETH every man that cometh into the world". I found this description of man in the Book of Instructions to be the exact truth. The real you—and I—are composed of LIGHT. When our bodies die we again become the original "LIGHT" we were before we entered our bodies—and then return to that "ZERO"—that great reservoir of LIGHT where we had our "beginning".

IT IS FINISHED